MARGINAL NOTES FOR THE OLD TESTAMENT

HELPS FOR TRANSLATORS SERIES

TECHNICAL HELPS:

Old Testament Quotations in the New Testament
Section Headings for the New Testament
Short Bible Reference System
New Testament Index
Orthography Studies
Bible Translations for Popular Use
*The Theory and Practice of Translation
Bible Index
Fauna and Flora of the Bible
Short Index to the Bible
Manuscript Preparation
Marginal Notes for the Old Testament
Marginal Notes for the New Testament

HANDBOOKS:

A Translator's Handbook on Ruth
A Translator's Handbook on the Book of Amos
A Translator's Handbook on the Book of Jonah
A Translator's Handbook on the Gospel of Mark
*A Translator's Handbook on the Gospel of Luke
A Translator's Handbook on the Gospel of John
A Translator's Handbook on the Acts of the Apostles
A Translator's Handbook on Paul's Letter to the Romans
A Translator's Handbook on Paul's Letter to the Galatians
A Translator's Handbook on Paul's Letter to the Philippians
A Translator's Handbook on Paul's Letters to the Colossians and to Philemon
A Translator's Handbook on Paul's Letters to the Thessalonians
A Translator's Handbook on the First Letter from Peter
A Translator's Handbook on the Letters of John

HELPS FOR TRANSLATORS

MARGINAL NOTES FOR THE OLD TESTAMENT

BASED ON THE TEXT OF TODAY'S ENGLISH VERSION

by
ROBERT G. BRATCHER

UNITED BIBLE SOCIETIES

London, New York,
Stuttgart

© 1980 by the United Bible Societies

All Rights Reserved.

No part of this book may be translated or repro-
duced in any form without the written permission
of the United Bible Societies.

PRINTED IN THE UNITED STATES OF AMERICA

Books in the series of Helps for Translators
that are marked with an asterisk (*) may
best be ordered from

   United Bible Societies
   D-7000 Stuttgart 1
   Postfach 755
   West Germany

All other books in the series may best be
ordered from

   American Bible Society
   1865 Broadway
   New York, N.Y. 10023
   U.S.A.

ISBN 0-8267-0025-X

ABS-1980-800-CM-1-C#08557

PROVIDING MARGINAL NOTES FOR BIBLE TRANSLATIONS

These Marginal Notes are intended to provide the kind of information that will enable the reader to understand more fully the text of the TEV, the Good News Bible. They are offered to translators as typical of what can and should be done in other languages. Since the TEV is the base for these notes, translators may find it necessary to make adjustments for translations in other languages, all of which present unique problems of their own. These Marginal Notes may be classified as follows:

1. Textual: the more important textual variants are listed; besides those already included in the TEV some others have been added.

2. Translational: translational alternatives are given, particularly for words and phrases usually deemed significant; some alternatives are given which do not appear in the TEV. In some cases the wording for both the textual and the translational notes has been changed from what it is in the TEV, in order to conform more closely to the style of the Notes as a whole.

3. Linguistic: play on words, popular etymologies, meaning of technical words and phrases.

4. Cultural: beliefs, customs, rituals, festivals.

5. People: identification and significance.

6. Historical events: identification and significance.

7. Places: identification (where possible) and significance. Location is usually given in terms of distance from Jerusalem (particularly in the Old Testament), on the assumption that most readers know more or less where Jerusalem is; sometimes, however, the distance is given from the location to which the place is related in the narrative. All distances are given in kilometers.

8. Dates: these conform to the Chronological Table in TEV.

9. References: to other passages in the Bible, particularly in the New Testament.

Notes of the first two types have the alternate texts or translations in ordinary print, while the explanation is underlined. Notes that are explanatory or give a definition, as in types 3 to 9, have the word or phrase underlined that is to be discussed, while the explanation is in ordinary print.

Two additional matters:

1. A dictionary style of definition (not a complete sentence) is generally employed.

2. In compiling these Notes I have consistently consulted: Revised Standard Version, Oxford Study Edition; New English Bible, Oxford Study Edition; Bible de Jérusalem (third edition); Traduction Oecuménique de la Bible; and New American Bible.

Robert G. Bratcher

ABBREVIATIONS OF BOOKS OF THE BIBLE

1,2 Chr	1,2 Chronicles	1,2 Kgs	1,2 Kings
Col	Colossians	Lam	Lamentations
1,2 Cor	1,2 Corinthians	Lev	Leviticus
Dan	Daniel	Mal	Malachi
Deut	Deuteronomy	Matt	Matthew
Eccl	Ecclesiastes	Neh	Nehemiah
Eph	Ephesians	Num	Numbers
Est	Esther	Phil	Philippians
Exo	Exodus	Prov	Proverbs
Ezek	Ezekiel	Psa	Psalms
Gal	Galatians	Rev	Revelation
Gen	Genesis	Rom	Romans
Hab	Habbakuk	1,2 Sam	1,2 Samuel
Hag	Haggai	Song	Song of Solomon
Heb	Hebrews	1,2 Thes	1,2 Thessalonians
Hos	Hosea	1,2 Tim	1,2 Timothy
Isa	Isaiah	Zech	Zechariah
Jer	Jeremiah	Zeph	Zephaniah
Josh	Joshua		

GENESIS

1.1   In the beginning, when God created the universe; or In the beginning God created the universe; or When God began to create the universe.

1.2   the power of God; or the spirit of God; or a wind from God; or an awesome wind.

1.5   Evening...and morning: day began at sunset and ended at the following sunset.

1.6-7   The water: of the ocean which covered all the earth (see verse 2). The water above it: the source of rain.

1.14   religious festivals; or seasons.

1.26   We: either an example of what is called "the plural of majesty" or else a reference to the heavenly council, which included other supernatural beings (see 3.22; Job 1.6).
    One ancient translation animals, domestic and wild; Hebrew domestic animals and all the earth.

2.3   by that day he had completed his creation; or on that day he completed his creation.

2.4   The LORD: where the Hebrew text has Yahweh, traditionally translated as Jehovah, this translation employs LORD with capital letters, following a usage which is widespread in English versions.

2.7   Ground...man: the Hebrew words for "man" ('adam) and "ground" ('adamah) are similar in sound.

2.9   knowledge of what is good and what is bad; or knowledge of everything.

2.13   Cush (in Mesopotamia); or Sudan.

2.17   what is good and what is bad; or everything.

2.20   The man named all the birds and all the animals: an indication that man had authority over all other created beings.

2.23   Woman...man: the Hebrew words for "woman" ('ishah) and "man" ('ish) are similar in sound.

3.5   like God; or like the gods.
      what is good and what is bad; or everything.

3.15 offspring; or descendants.
      their; or his.

3.17 the man; or Adam.

3.20 Adam; or The man. The word 'adam in Hebrew means "mankind" (see
      1.26) or "man" (see 3.9,17).
          Eve: this name sounds similar to the Hebrew word for "living,"
      which is rendered in this context as "human beings."

3.22 what is good and what is bad; or everything.

3.24 Living creatures: thought of as having several wings and faces
      (see Ezek 1.5-12; 10.21), these creatures symbolized God's majesty
      and power.

4.1   Cain: this name sounds like the Hebrew for "gotten."

4.7   you would be smiling; or I would have accepted your offering.
      Sin is crouching: like a demon, ready to spring upon its victim.

4.8   Some ancient translations Let's go out in the fields; Hebrew does
      not have these words.

4.16 Went away from the LORD's presence: it was believed that a god's
      sovereignty extended only over the land that was his; by going to
      another land Cain was no longer in the Lord's presence (see 1 Sam
      26.19).

4.25 Seth: this name sounds like the Hebrew for "has given."

4.26 The LORD's holy name: Yahweh (see Exo 3.13-15).

5.2   Mankind; or Man, or Adam (see 3.20).

5.29 Noah: this name sounds like the Hebrew for "relief."

6.2   supernatural beings; or sons of the gods; or sons of God.

6.16 roof; or window.

6.18 Covenant: a promise that God makes to protect and bless those who
      obey him.
      Your sons: Shem, Ham, and Japheth (see 5.32).

7.11 Second month: Ziv, the Jewish month that began with the first new
      moon occurring after the modern April 10.
      Floodgates of the sky: holding back the waters above (see 1.6-8).

8.2   Floodgates of the sky: see 7.11.

8.4   Seventh month: Tishri, the Jewish month that began with the first new moon occurring after the modern September 4.
     The Ararat range: in what later became Armenia (now a part of Turkey).

8.5   Tenth month: Tebeth, the Jewish month that began with the first new moon occurring in modern December.

8.13   First month: Abib, the Jewish month that began with the first new moon occurring after the modern March 11.

8.14   Second month: see 7.11.

9.13   Bow: the rainbow was regarded as God's weapon with which he shot his arrows, the flashes of lightning (see Hab 3.9).

9.27   Japheth: this name sounds like the Hebrew for "increase."

10.14   Probable text and of Crete...descended; Hebrew from whom the Philistines are descended, and Crete.

10.25   Peleg: this name sounds like the Hebrew for "divide."

11.7   Us: see 1.26.

11.9   Babylon: this name sounds like the Hebrew for "mixed up."

12.3   And through you I will bless all the nations; or All nations will ask me to bless them as I have blessed you.

12.6   Shechem: a city some 50 kilometers north of Jerusalem.

12.8   Bethel: a city some 19 kilometers north of Jerusalem; Ai was 3 kilometers east of Bethel.

13.3   Bethel and Ai: see 12.8.

13.10   Zoar: at the southeastern end of the Dead Sea.
     Garden of the Lord: a reference to the Garden of Eden.

13.18   Hebron: a city some 32 kilometers southwest of Jerusalem.

14.14   Dan: a city some 40 kilometers north of Lake Galilee.

14.17   King's Valley: near Jerusalem (see 2 Sam 18.18).

14.18   Salem: a name for Jerusalem.

15.2   Probable text My only heir is Eliezer of Damascus; Hebrew unclear.

15.18   Covenant: see 6.18.

16.2   A child for me: the child borne by a slave girl would be regarded as the child of her mistress.

16.3   Concubine: a female servant who, although not a wife, had sexual relations with her master. She had important legal rights, and her master was referred to as her husband.

16.5   It's your fault that Hagar despises me; or May you suffer for this wrong done against me.

16.7   Shur: on the Egyptian border; Hagar was Egyptian (verse 1).

16.11   Ishmael: this name in Hebrew means "God hears."

16.13   Probable text lived to tell about it?; Hebrew unclear.

17.5   Abram: this name in Hebrew means "famous ancestor."
        Abraham: this name sounds like the Hebrew for "ancestor of many nations."

17.7   Covenant: see 6.18.

17.10   Circumcise: to cut off the foreskin of the penis.

17.15   Sarah: this name in Hebrew means "princess."

17.19   Isaac: this name in Hebrew means "he laughs" (see verse 17).

18.1   Mamre: see 13.18.

18.10   Nine months from now; or This time next year.

18.18   through him I will bless all the nations; or all the nations will ask me to bless them as I have blessed him.

19.22   Zoar: this name sounds like the Hebrew for "small" (see 13.10).

19.27   Where he had stood: see 18.16.

19.31   the whole world; or this land.

19.37   Moab: this name sounds like the Hebrew for "from my father."

19.38   Benammi: this name in Hebrew means "son of my relative" and sounds like the Hebrew for "Ammonite."

20.1   Gerar: in southwest Judah, near the Philistine border, some 80 kilometers west of the Dead Sea.

20.7   Prophet: here in the sense of one who speaks for God and so is able to intercede with him on behalf of someone else.

21.4   Circumcised: see 17.10.

21.6   Laughter: the name Isaac in Hebrew means "he laughs" (see 17.17-19).

21.9   playing with; or making fun of.
Some ancient translations with Sarah's son Isaac; Hebrew does not have these words.

21.14   Beersheba: in the southern part of the country.

21.16   Hebrew she; one ancient translation the child.

21.20   Wilderness of Paran: in the northeast region of the Sinai Peninsula.

21.22   Abimelech: see 20.2.

21.31   Beersheba: this name in Hebrew means "Well of the Vow" or "Well of Seven" (see 26.33).

22.14   Provides; or Sees.
provides; or is seen.

22.24   Concubine: see 16.3.

23.19   Buried his wife in that cave: where Abraham himself was later buried (25.9-10), Isaac and Rebecca (49.31), Jacob (50.13) and Leah (49.31).

24.2   Place your hand between my thighs: this was the way in which a vow was made absolutely unchangeable.

24.62   Some ancient translations into the wilderness of; Hebrew from coming.
"The Well of the Living One Who Sees Me": see 16.14.

25.22   Went to ask: at the sanctuary, where the Lord was worshiped.

25.25   Esau: this name is taken to refer to Seir, the territory later inhabited by Esau's descendants; Seir sounds like the Hebrew for "hairy."

25.26   Jacob: this name sounds like the Hebrew for "heel."

25.30   Edom: this name sounds like the Hebrew for "red."

25.31   rights as the first-born son: to be the future head of the family, and to receive a share of the father's estate twice as large as that of any other surviving son.

26.1   The earlier one: see 12.10.
Abimelech...at Gerar: see 20.2.

26.23   Beersheba: see 22.19.

26.33   Beersheba: this name in Hebrew means "Well of the Vow" or "Well of Seven" (see 21.31).

27.36   Jacob: this name sounds like the Hebrew for "cheat" (see also 25.26).

27.40   rebel; or grow restless.

28.11   a holy place; or a place.

28.13   beside him; or on it.

28.14   through you and your descendants I will bless all the nations; or all the nations will ask me to bless them as I have blessed you and your descendants.

28.19   Bethel: this name in Hebrew means "house of God."

29.13   Everything that had happened: between himself and Esau.

29.17   lovely; or weak.

29.32   Reuben: this name sounds like the Hebrew for "see, a son" and "has seen my trouble."

29.33   Simeon: this name sounds like the Hebrew for "hear."

29.34   Levi: this name sounds like the Hebrew for "bound."

29.35   Judah: this name sounds like the Hebrew for "praise."

30.3   A child for me: see 16.2.

30.6   Dan: this name sounds like the Hebrew for "judge in favor."

30.8   Naphtali: this name sounds like the Hebrew for "fight."

30.11   Gad: this name in Hebrew means "luck."

30.13   Asher: this name in Hebrew means "happy."

30.14   Mandrakes: plants which were believed to produce fertility and were used as love charms.

30.18   Issachar: this name sounds like the Hebrew for "a man is hired" and "there is reward."

30.20   Zebulun: this name sounds like the Hebrew for "accept" and "gift."

30.24   Joseph: this name sounds like the Hebrew for "may he give another" and "he has taken away."

30.30   wherever I went; or because of me.

30.32   One ancient translation every black lamb; Hebrew every spotted
and speckled lamb, and every black lamb.
Every black lamb and every spotted or speckled young goat: lambs
were usually white and goats were usually black, so the bargain
seems to be all in Laban's favor.

30.39   They produced young that were streaked, speckled, and spotted: it
was believed that the coloration of the young was determined by what
the mother animal was looking at at the time of conception.

31.21   Gilead: on the east side of the Jordan River.

31.33   The two slave women: Zilpah (29.24) and Bilhah (29.29).

31.42   the God of...Isaac: or the Kinsman of...Isaac.

31.47   Laban...Jacob: Laban spoke Aramaic; Jacob spoke Hebrew.
Jegar Sahadutha: this name in Aramaic means "a pile to remind us."
Galeed: this name in Hebrew means "a pile to remind us."

31.49   Mizpah: this name sounds like the Hebrew for "place from which
to watch."

31.53   Abraham...Nahor: Abraham was Jacob's grandfather and Nahor was
Laban's father.

32.2   Mahanaim: this name in Hebrew means "two camps."

32.3   Edom: south of the Dead Sea.

32.22   His two concubines: Zilpah (29.24) and Bilhah (29.29); and see
16.3.
The Jabbok River: a tributary of the Jordan River, on the east
side of the river.

32.28   Israel: this name sounds like the Hebrew for "he struggles with
God" or "God struggles."

32.30   Peniel: this name sounds like the Hebrew for "the face of God."

32.32   Today: the time of the writing of the account.

33.1   The two concubines: see 32.22.

33.15   for I only want to gain your favor; or if it's all right with you.

33.17   Sukkoth: this name in Hebrew means "shelters."

33.18   Shechem: see 12.6.

34.3   tried to win her affection; or comforted her.

34.14   Circumcised: see 17.10.

(7)

35.3 Purify yourselves: a ritual to remove any ceremonial impurity which prevented the proper performance of religious duties.

35.6 Bethel: some 19 kilometers north of Jerusalem.

35.8 Rebecca's nurse: see 24.59.

35.18 Benoni: this name in Hebrew means "son of my sorrow."
Benjamin: this name in Hebrew means "son who will be fortunate" or "son who will live in the south."

35.19 Bethlehem: some 8 kilometers south of Jerusalem.

35.20 This day: the time of the writing of the account.

35.22 Concubines; see 16.3.
One ancient translation and was furious; Hebrew does not have these words.

36.2 Some ancient translations son; Hebrew daughter or granddaughter.

36.14 Some ancient translations son; Hebrew daughter or granddaughter.

37.2 Concubines: see 16.3.

37.3 robe with full sleeves; or decorated robe.

37.17 Dothan: some 25 kilometers north of Shechem.

37.23 robe with full sleeves; or decorated robe.

37.28 Probable text the brothers; Hebrew they (that is, the Midianites).

38.1 Adullam: not far from Bethlehem.

38.8 Your brother may have descendants: the first son born to a widow and her brother-in-law would be regarded as the dead man's child (see Deut 25.5-6).

38.18 Seal; a ring or a cylinder used to stamp one's signature; it was held by a cord around the neck.

38.29 Perez; this name in Hebrew means "breaking out." He was one of King David's ancestors (see Ruth 4.18; Matt 1.3).
Zerah; apparently this name is somehow related to a Hebrew word for "red."

41.51 Manasseh; this name sounds like the Hebrew for "cause to forget."

41.52 Ephraim; this name sounds like the Hebrew for "give children."

44.5 One ancient translation Why did you steal my master's silver cup?; Hebrew does not have these words.

45.10 Goshen: in the eastern part of the Nile Delta.

46.1   Beersheba: where Isaac had built an altar to God (see 26.23-25; 28.10).

46.12 Er and Onan had died: see 38.7,10.

46.27 Seventy the total number: this includes Joseph and his two sons born in Egypt, and Jacob himself.

47.29 Place your hand between my thighs: see 24.2.

47.30 Where my fathers are: in the cave at Machpelah (see 23.19; 49.31; 50.13).

48.3   Luz: that is, Bethel (see 28.10-19).

48.14 Right hand: regarded as more powerful and of greater benefit than the left hand.

48.15 Joseph: by blessing Ephraim and Manasseh, Jacob was blessing Joseph.

49.4   You slept with my concubine: see 35.22.

49.10 Probable text Nations will bring him tribute; Hebrew unclear.

49.12 His eyes...milk; or His eyes are darker than wine, his teeth are whiter than milk.

49.13 Sidon: a Phoenician city on the Mediterranean coast, north of Palestine.

49.21 Naphtali...fawns; or Naphtali is a spreading tree that puts out lovely branches.

49.22 Joseph...hillside; or Joseph is like a tree by a spring, a fruitful tree that spreads over a wall.

49.24 But...strong; or But their bows were broken and splintered, the muscles of their arms torn apart.

49.26 Probable text grain and flowers; Hebrew your fathers are mightier than.
       One ancient translation ancient mountains; Hebrew my ancestors to.

49.29 The cave: see 23.17-20.

50.8   Goshen: see 45.10; 47.6.

50.11 Abel Mizraim: this name sounds like the Hebrew for "mourning of the Egyptians."

EXODUS

1.5   Seventy: see Gen 46.27.

1.10   escape from; or take control of.

2.4   Sister: Miriam (see Num 26.59).

2.10   Moses: this name sounds like the Hebrew for "pull out."

2.15-16   Midian: east of the Gulf of Aqaba.

2.22   Gershom: this name sounds like the Hebrew for "foreigner."

2.24   Covenant: a promise that God makes to protect and bless those who obey him; with Abraham: see Gen 12.1-3; Isaac: see Gen 26.2-5; Jacob: see Gen 28.13-15.

3.14   I am who I am...I AM; or I will be who I will be...I WILL BE. "I am" sounds like the Hebrew name Yahweh (or, Jehovah), which is represented in this translation by "the LORD."

4.20   Sons: Gershom (2.22) and Eliezer (18.3-4).

4.25-26   Feet: probably a euphemism for the genitals. Circumcision: the ritual of cutting off the foreskin of the penis.

4.27   The holy mountain: Sinai (see 3.1).

5.7   Straw: it was cut into small pieces and added to the wet molded clay to make it keep its shape while it was drying.

6.3   Almighty God: a translation of the Hebrew 'el-shadai, which probably means "God of the Mountain" (see Gen 17.1). The LORD: see 3.14. Where the Hebrew text has Yahweh, tradition-ally transliterated as Jehovah, this translation employs LORD with capital letters, following a usage which is widespread in English versions.

6.5   My covenant: see 2.24.

8.22   Goshen: see Gen 47.6.

8.23   Some ancient translations a distinction; Hebrew redemption.

8.26   Would be offended: because the Israelites would be sacrificing animals that were considered sacred by the Egyptians.

9.32   It ripens later: in late March or early April, about one month after the flax and the barley (verse 31).

10.19   Gulf of Suez: see Red Sea in 13.18.

12.2   First month of the year: Abib, the Jewish month that began with the first new moon occurring after the modern March 11.

12.6   On the evening of the fourteenth day of the month: the night of full moon.

12.8   Bitter herbs: such as endive, chicory, dandelion, and sorrell.

12.18   The first month: see 12.2.

12.22   dip it in the bowl containing; or put it on the threshold covered with.

12.37   Sukkoth: about 50 kilometers southeast of Rameses.

12.44   Circumcise: see 4.25-26.

13.4   First month: see 12.2,

13.17   Philistia: on the Mediterranean coast, west of Canaan.

13.18   Red Sea: (in Hebrew literally "Sea of Reeds") evidently referred originally to (1) a series of lakes and marshes between the head of the Gulf of Suez and the mediterranean, the region generally regarded as the site of the events described in Exodus 14, and was extended to include (2) the Gulf of Suez, and (3) the Gulf of Aqaba.

13.19   Promise: see Gen 50.25.

14.8   triumphantly; or under the protection of the Lord.

14.20   Probable text The cloud...Israel; Hebrew unclear.

15.4   Red Sea: see 13.18.

15.13   Your sacred land: Canaan.

15.17   The place that you, LORD, have chosen: Jerusalem.

15.20   Tambourine: a small drum with pieces of metal in the rim, held in one hand and shaken.

15.23   Marah: this name in Hebrew means "bitter."

16.1   The second month: Ziv, the Jewish month that began with the first new moon occurring after the modern April 10.

16.31   Manna: this word sounds like the Hebrew for "what is it?" (see verse 15).

16.34   The Covenant Box: see 25.10-22.

16.35   Ate manna for the next fifty years: see Josh 5.11-12.

17.7   Massah...Meribah: these names in Hebrew mean "testing" and "complaining."

17.8   Amalekites: a desert tribe.

17.16   Probable text Hold high the banner of the Lord!; Hebrew unclear.

18.3   Gershom: this name sounds like the Hebrew for "foreigner" (see 2.22).

18.4   Eliezer: this name sounds like the Hebrew for "God helps me."

18.5   The holy mountain: see 4.27.

19.1-2 The third month: Sivan, the Jewish month that began with the first new moon occurring after the modern May 9.

19.5   My covenant: see 2.24.

19.10   Purifying themselves: performing a ritual to remove any ceremonial impurity which prevented the proper performance of religious duties.

20.4   Water under the earth: the vast subterranean ocean, the source of springs and fountains (see Gen 1.6-8; 7.11).

20.6   thousands of generations; or thousands.

20.24   Fellowship offerings: sacrifices in which only a part of the animal was burned on the altar; the rest was eaten by the worshipers.

20.26   You will expose yourselves: apparently the man offering the sacrifice wore only a cloth around his waist.

21.8   because he has treated her unfairly; or because this would be unfair to her.

21.18   his fist; or a hoe.

22.5   If...crops; or If a man burns off a field or a vineyard, and lets the fire get out of control and burn up the crops.

22.28   God; or the judges.

22.31   Animal that has been killed by wild animals: not ritually pure because the blood had not been properly drained out (see Lev 17.10-12).

23.15   Abib: the Jewish month that began with the first new moon occurring after the modern March 11.

23.16   The Harvest Festival: held fifty days after Passover, around the eighth day of Sivan, the third Jewish month, which began with the first new moon occurring after the modern May 9.
Festival of Shelters: a seven-day festival, beginning on the fifteenth day of Tishri, the seventh Jewish month, which began with the first new moon occurring after the modern September 4.

23.19   In its mother's milk: a method used by Canaanites in their fertility rites.

23.24   Sacred stone pillars: symbols of Baal, the Canaanite god of fertility.

23.28   I will throw your enemies into panic; or I will send hornets among your enemies.

24.7   The book of the covenant: a reference to the laws written down by Moses (verse 4).

24.8   The covenant: see 2.24.

24.9   Nadab, Abihu: Aaron's sons (see 6.23).

24.13   Hebrew Moses began; one ancient translation they began.

25.7   Ephod: in most instances the word refers to a type of shoulder garment which, in certain respects, resembled a vest. To it was attached a kind of pouch containing the Urim and Thummim, two objects used in determining God's will. See the description in 28.6-12.

25.18   Winged creatures: symbols of God's majesty and associated with his presence; for a description of them see also Ezek 1.5-12; 10.21.

26.1   Tent of my presence: the place of worship, where God met his people; it was used until Solomon built the Temple in Jerusalem.

26.31   Winged creatures: see 25.18.

27.2   Projections: located at the top corners of the altar (see 29.12); anyone who took hold of them could escape punishment for his crime (see 1 Kgs 1.50; 2.28).

28.4   Ephod: see 25.7.

28.30   Urim and Thummim: two objects used by the priest to determine God's will; it is not known precisely how they were used.

28.35   He will not be killed: it was believed that the sound of the bells would frighten off any evil spiritual beings which might be lurking near by.

29.4   Tent of my presence: see 26.1.

29.37   The power of its holiness: it was believed that ordinary persons or things would be harmed by coming in contact with something holy.

29.39   The morning...the evening: the traditional hours were 9:00 A.M. and 3:00 P.M.

(13)

30.10   Once a year: on the Day of Atonement, the tenth day of Tishri, the seventh Jewish month, which began with the first new moon occurring after the modern September 4.

30.29   The power of its holiness: see 29.37.

31.3   power; or spirit.

31.16   The covenant: see 2.24.

32.1   a god; or some gods.

32.20   Water: from the stream that flowed down Mount Sinai (see Deut 9.21).

32.29   Some ancient translations Today you have consecrated yourselves; Hebrew Consecrate yourselves today.

33.19   My sacred name: see 3.14.

34.5   His holy name: see 3.14.

34.7   thousands of generations; or thousands.

34.13   Sacred pillars: see 23.24.
        Asherah: a Canaanite goddess of fertility; her male counterpart was Baal.

34.18   Abib: see 23.15.

34.22   Harvest Festival: see 23.16.
        Festival of Shelters: see 23.16.

34.25   Passover Festival: see 12.1-14.

34.26   Its mother's milk: see 23.19.

35.9   Ephod: see 25.7.

35.31   power; or spirit.

37.7   Winged creatures: see 25.18.

38.2   Projections: see 27.2.

39.2   Ephod: see 25.7.

40.2   First month: Abib (see 23.15).

40.17   After they left Egypt: almost one year later, and exactly nine months after arriving at Sinai (19.1-2).

LEVITICUS

1.1   Tent of the LORD's presence: the place of worship, where God met his people (see Exo 26); it was used until Solomon built the Temple in Jerusalem.

1.3   Burnt offering: a sacrifice in which the whole animal (except for its hide) was burned on the altar.
        him; or it.

1.14   A bird: people who were not rich enough to be able to offer an animal (verses 2-13) could offer a bird instead.

2.1   Incense: material which produces a pleasant smell when burned.

3.1   Fellowship offering: an offering in which only a part of the animal was burned on the altar; the rest was eaten by the worshipers.

3.2   Tent of the LORD's presence: see 1.1.

4.4   The Tent: see 1.1.

4.6   Sacred curtain: separating the Holy Place from the Most Holy Place (see Exo 26.31-33).

4.7   Projections: located at the top corners of the altar (see Exo 30.1-3).

4.31   Fellowship offerings: see 3.1.

5.7   Cannot afford: this section (verses 7-13) supplements the section 4.27-35, which covers the case of sins committed by the common people.

6.16-17 Tent of the LORD's presence: see 1.1.

6.18   Power of its holiness: it was believed that ordinary persons or things would be harmed by coming in contact with something holy.

6.20   The morning...the evening: the traditional hours were 9:00 A.M. and 3:00 P.M.

7.11   Fellowship offerings: see 3.1.

8.1   Tent of my presence: see 1.1.

8.7   Ephod: a type of shoulder garment which, in certain respects, resembled a vest; to it was attached a kind of pouch containing the Urim and Thummim (see Exo 28.6-12).

8.8   Urim and Thummim: two objects used by the priest to determine God's will; it is not known precisely how they were used.

(15)

8.15   Projections: see 4.7.

9.5   Tent: see 1.1.

9.9   Projections: see 4.7.

9.18   Fellowship offering: see 3.1.

9.22   Stepped down: from the altar.

9.24   The LORD sent a fire: to demonstrate that he accepted the sacrifices.

10.1   Nadab and Abihu: Aaron's two oldest sons (see Exo 6.23).

10.2   The LORD sent fire: as punishment.

10.3   Who serve me: as priests.
I will reveal my glory to my people; or my people must honor me.
remained silent; or broke into a lament.

10.5   Sacred Tent: see 1.1.

10.14   Fellowship offerings: see 3.1.

11.13-19   Cormorants: the identification of some of the birds in verses 13-19 is uncertain.

12.4   Sacred Tent: see 1.1.

13.2   Dreaded skin disease: traditionally thought of as leprosy; the Hebrew word, however, included other skin diseases as well (and see 13.47).

13.47   Mildew: the same Hebrew word means both "dreaded skin disease" and "mildew."

14.1   Dreaded skin disease: see 13.2.

14.11   Tent of the LORD's presence: see 1.1.

14.34   Mildew: see 13.47.

16.1   Who were killed: see 10.1-2.

16.2   Proper time: see verse 29.
Most Holy Place: the innermost part of the Tent of the LORD's Presence, where the Covenant Box was kept (see Exo 26.31-35).
Covenant Box: see Exo 25.10-22.

16.8   Azazel: the meaning of this Hebrew proper noun is unknown; it may be the name of a desert demon.

16.18   Projections: see 4.7.

16.20   Azazel: see 16.8.

16.29   Seventh month: Tishri, the Jewish month that began with the first
new moon occurring after the modern September 4.

16.34   Moses; or Aaron.

17.5   Fellowship offerings: see 3.1.

17.15   Died a natural death or has been killed by wild animals: the
blood of such an animal had not been properly drained out and so
the animal could not be eaten.

18.21   Molech: the god of the Ammonites (see 1 Kgs 11.7).

19.5   Fellowship offering: see 3.1.

19.14   a deaf man; or someone who cannot talk.

19.17   so...him; or so that you do not commit this sin against him.

19.18   Love your neighbor as you love yourself: the commandment which
Jesus called the second most important (see Mark 12.31).
Neighbor: fellow Israelite.

19.20   Concubine: a female servant who, although not a wife, had sexual
relations with her master. She had important legal rights, and her
master was referred to as her husband.
they will be punished, but not put to death; or an investigation
will be made, but they will not be put to death.

19.24   show your gratitude to me; or in praise of me.

19.28   To mourn for the dead: all these rites (verses 27-28) were
practiced by the Canaanites and were considered pagan.

19.29   Temple prostitutes: these women were found in Canaanite Temples,
where fertility gods were worshiped. It was believed that intercourse with these prostitutes assured fertile fields and herds.

20.2   Molech: see 18.21.

21.4   Verse 4 in Hebrew is unclear.

21.5   In mourning: see 19.28.

21.20   Eunuch: a man physically incapable of having sexual intercourse.

21.23   Sacred curtain: see 4.6.

22.4   Dreaded skin disease: see 13.2.

22.8   Any animal: see 17.15.

22.21   Fellowship offering: see 3.1.

23.5   Passover: the festival which celebrated the deliverance of the
ancient Hebrews from their captivity in Egypt (see Exo 12.21-27).
First month: Abib (later called Nisan), the Jewish month that
began with the first new moon occurring after the modern March 11.

23.6   Unleavened Bread: the festival which also celebrated the deliverance of the ancient Hebrews from their captivity in Egypt (see
Exo 12.15-20).

23.9-10 Grain: barley, which ripened in April.

23.15   Grain: wheat.

23.16   Fiftieth day: the reason why the Harvest Festival was also known
as Pentecost (from the Greek word for "fiftieth").

23.23-24 Seventh month: see 16.29.

23.26-27 Annual ritual: the Jewish name of the Day of Atonement is
Yom Kippur.

23.32   Sunset: the time at which the Jewish day began.

24.3   Covenant Box: see Exo 25.10-22.
Most Holy Place: see 16.2.

24.5   Twelve loaves: one for each of the twelve Israelite tribes.

25.9   Day of Atonement: see 23.26-32.

25.33   Probable text If a house...Restoration; Hebrew unclear.

26.9   Covenant: the promise that God made to his people to protect
and bless them if they obeyed him.

27.2   Given to the LORD: for service at the place of worship.

27.28   Unconditionally dedicated: anything dedicated in this way belonged
completely to the LORD and could not be used; it had to be destroyed.

NUMBERS

1.1   Second month: Ziv, the Jewish month that began with the first new
moon that occurred after the modern April 10.
   Left Egypt: see Exo 12.40-42.
   Tent of his presence: the place of worship, where God met his
people (see Exo 26); it was used until Solomon built the Temple in
Jerusalem.

3.4   Were killed: see Lev 10.1-2.

3.31   Covenant Box: see Exo 25.10-22.
   The curtain: separating the Holy Place from the Most Holy Place
(see Exo 26.31-33).

3.39   22,000: the total of the figures in verses 22,28,34 is actually
22,300.

4.19   Be killed: it was believed that ordinary persons or things would
be harmed by coming in contact with something holy (see Exo 29.37).

4.20   see...moving; or see the sacred objects even for a moment.

5.2   Dreaded skin disease: traditionally thought of as leprosy; the
Hebrew word, however, included other skin diseases as well.

5.17   Tent of the LORD's presence: see 1.1.

6.2   Nazirite: one who took a vow to dedicate himself to the LORD,
either for a limited time or indefinitely.

6.17   Fellowship offering: an offering in which only a part of the
animal was burned on the altar; the rest was eaten by the worshipers.

7.1   The day: see Exo 40.17.

7.89   Covenant Box: see 3.31.
   Winged creatures: symbols of God's majesty and associated with
his presence (see Exo 25.18-20); for a description of them see
Ezek 1.5-12;10.21).

8.4   The pattern: see Exo 25.31-40.

8.6   Purify: remove all ceremonial defilement by means of a ritual.

8.19   Disasters...if they came too near: see 4.19.

9.1   First month: Abib (later called Nisan), the Jewish month that
began with the first new moon occurring after the modern March 11.

9.2-3   Passover: the festival which celebrated the deliverance of the
ancient Hebrews from their captivity in Egypt (see Exo 12.21-27).

9.11   Second month: see 1.1.
          Bitter herbs: such as endive, chicory, dandelion, and sorrell.

9.12   The animal: either a lamb or a young goat (see Exo 12.3-5).

9.15-16   The day: see Exo 40.17.

10.11   Second month: see 1.1.

10.12   Started on their journey: the Israelites had been at Sinai eleven
          months (see Exo 19.1-2); they departed nineteen days after the
          census (see Num 1.1).
          Wilderness of Paran: north of Mount Sinai.

10.36   Return...Israel; or Return, LORD, you who are like an army of
          millions for Israel.

11.3   Taberah: this name sounds like the Hebrew for "burning."

11.4   Foreigners: see in Exo 12.38 the mention of "a large number of
          other people."

11.6   This manna: see Exo 16.13-16,31.

11.18   Purify yourselves: see 8.6.

11.31   The sea: probably the Gulf of Aqaba.
          sea, flying...direction; or sea. They settled in the camp and all
          around it for miles and miles in every direction, until they were
          piled up three feet deep on the ground.

12.1   Cushite; or Midianite (see Hab 3.7); or Sudanese.

12.2   through; or to.

12.6   Some ancient translations when there are prophets among you;
          Hebrew unclear.

12.7   I have put him in charge of my people Israel; or he can be
          trusted with all my affairs.

12.10   Dreaded disease: see 5.2.

12.16   Wilderness of Paran: see 10.12.

13.16   Hoshea...Joshua: two forms of the same name, which in Hebrew
          means "The LORD saves"; in Greek the name becomes "Jesus"
          (see Matt 1.21).

13.20   The season: about the middle or end of July.

13.22   Hebron: some 32 kilometers south of Jerusalem.

13.24   Eshcol: this name in Hebrew means "bunch of grapes."

13.25   Kadesh: also known as Kadesh Barnea, an oasis some 145 kilometers northwest of the northern end of the Gulf of Aqaba.

13.30   complaining against; or gathered around.

14.17-18   You said: see Exo 34.6-7.

14.34   to have me against you; or to oppose me.

14.45   Hormah: in the southern part of Canaan, some 80 kilometers northeast of Kadesh.

15.15   Some ancient translations the same; Hebrew the congregation the same.

15.38   Tassels: ornaments made of threads or cords bound at one end.

16.19   Korah gathered the whole community; or Korah gathered all his followers.

16.30   The world of the dead: called Sheol; it was thought of as a vast abyss in the depths of the earth.

18.7   Most Holy Place: the innermost part of the Tent of the LORD's presence, where the Covenant Box was kept (see Exo 26.31-35).

18.14   Unconditionally dedicated: anything dedicated in this way belonged completely to the LORD and could not be used for ordinary purposes; in some instances it had to be destroyed (see 21.2).

18.21   Tithe: one-tenth of the whole.

19.3   It...presence; or He is to take it outside to the east of the camp and kill it.

19.15   no lid; or no lid fastened.

20.1   First month: Abib (later called Nisan), the Jewish month that began with the first new moon occurring after the modern March 11; contrary to general usage, the year is not given here.
Wilderness of Zin: southwest of the Dead Sea.
Kadesh: see 13.25.

20.13   Meribah: this name in Hebrew means "complaining."

20.14   Edom: the land to the south of the Dead Sea.
Your kinsmen: the people of Edom were descended from Esau, the brother of Jacob, who was the ancestor of the Israelites.

20.17   Main road: the route east of the Dead Sea, going from Elath, on the northern end of the Gulf of Aqaba, all the way north to Syria.
main road; or King's Highway.

20.22   Mount Hor: precise location unknown.

21.2   Unconditionally dedicate: see 18.14.

21.3   Hormah: this name in Hebrew means "destruction."

21.13   Arnon River: flowing from east to west into the east side of the Dead Sea.

21.14   Book of the LORD's Battles: a book, no longer in existence, of Hebrew songs.

21.20   Mount Pisgah: about 15 kilometers east of the northern end of the Dead Sea.

21.22   Main road: see 20.17.
main road; or King's Highway.

21.24   The Jabbok: a river on the east side of the Jordan which flowed into the Jordan River some 50 kilometers north of the Dead Sea.

21.25   Heshbon: about 10 kilometers east of Mount Pisgah.

21.28   One ancient translation devoured; Hebrew the lords of.

21.29   Chemosh: the god of the Moabites.

21.30   Verse 30 in Hebrew is unclear.

21.33   Bashan: a region northeast of Lake Galilee.

22.32   Probable text you should not be making this journey; Hebrew unclear.

23.7   Syria; or Mesopotamia.

23.14   Mount Pisgah: see 21.20.

23.23   There...Israel; or No magic charms are used in Israel, no witchcraft is practiced there.

23.28   Mount Peor: about 5 kilometers northwest of Mount Pisgah.

24.3   who can see clearly; or whose eyes are closed.

24.7   One ancient translation They...fields; Hebrew unclear.

24.15   who can see clearly; or whose eyes are closed.

24.17   the people of Seth; or who are proud and violent.

24.22   Verse 22 in Hebrew is unclear.

24.23   Probable text Who...north; Hebrew unclear.

25.1   Acacia Valley: northeast of the Dead Sea.

25.4   in broad daylight; or publicly.

26.9   Dathan and Abiram...Korah: see 16.1-35.

26.21   Er and Onan: see Gen 38.6-10.

26.61   Nadab and Abihu: see 3.4.

27.12   Mount Abarim: a chain of hills to the east of the northern end of the Dead Sea.

27.21   Urim and Thummim: two objects used by the priest to determine God's will; it is not known precisely how they were used.

28.4   Morning...evening: the traditional hours were 9:00 A.M. and 3:00 P.M.

28.16   Passover Festival: see 9.2-3.
        First month: see 9.1.

28.26   Harvest Festival: 50 days after Passover (see Lev 23.15-16).

29.1   Seventh month: Tishri, the Jewish month that began with the first new moon occurring after the modern September 4.

31.2   What they did: see 25.16-18.

31.16   At Peor: see 25.1-9.

31.23   The water for purification: see 19.9.

32.1   Jazer and Gilead: on the east side of the Jordan River.

32.5   Cross: to the west side.

32.8   To explore the land: see 13.17-24.

33.3   First month: see 9.1.

33.8   Red Sea: (in Hebrew literally "Sea of Reeds") evidently referred originally to (1) a series of lakes and marshes between the head of the Gulf of Suez and the Mediterranean, the region generally regarded as the site of the events described in Exodus 14, and was extended to include (2) the Gulf of Suez (see Exo 10.19), and (3) the Gulf of Aqaba (see Exo 23.31).

33.37   Mount Hor: see 20.22.

33.38-39   Fifth month: Ab, the Jewish month that began with the first new moon occurring after the modern July 7.

34.7   Mount Hor: in the north; not the one on which Aaron died (33.38-39).

36.4   The Year of Restoration: see Lev 25.8-17.

DEUTERONOMY

1.3   Eleventh month: Shebat, the Jewish month that began with the first new moon occurring in modern January.

1.4   The LORD; or Moses.

2.8   Elath: also known as Eziongeber, a port town at the northern end of the Gulf of Aqaba.

2.13   Zered River: the northern frontier of Edom, flowing into the southeastern end of the Dead Sea.

2.24   Arnon River: flowing from east to west into the east side of the Dead Sea.

2.37   Jabbok River: the western border of Ammon (see 3.16).

3.8   Arnon River: see 2.24.
        Mount Hermon: at the northern end of the land, near Syria.

3.11   Rephaim: a race of giants (see 2.10-11).
        coffin; or bed.
        stone; or iron.
        Still be seen: at the time of the writing of the account.

3.27   Mount Pisgah: about 15 kilometers east of the northern end of the Dead Sea.

4.3   What the LORD did: see Num 25.1-9.
        Baal: a fertility god of the Canaanites.

4.10   Sinai; or Horeb.

4.48   One ancient translation Sirion; Hebrew Sion.

5.8   Water under the earth: the vast subterranean ocean, the source of springs and fountains (see Gen 1.6-8; 7.11).

5.10   thousands of generations; or thousands.

6.4   The LORD...is our God; or The LORD, our God, is the only God; or The LORD our God is one.

6.5   Love the LORD: the commandment which Jesus called the most important of all (see Mark 12.29-30).

6.16   Massah: see Exo 17.1-7.

6.25   If we faithfully...with us; or The right thing for us to do is to obey faithfully everything that God has commanded us.

7.5   Asherah: a fertility goddess of the Canaanites; her male counterpart was Baal.

7.20   cause panic; or send hornets; or send plagues.

8.3   Gave you manna: see Exo 16.13-35.

8.15   He made water flow out: see Num 20.2-11.

9.9   The covenant: the Ten Commandments.

9.22   Taberah: see Num 11.1-3.
       Massah: see Exo 17.1-7.
       Kibroth Hattavah: see Num 11.33-34.

10.6   Aaron died: see Num 20.22-28.

10.8   the mountain; or that time.
       Covenant Box: see Exo 25.10-22.

10.22 Seventy: see Gen 46.26-27; Exo 1.5.

11.4   Red Sea: (in Hebrew literally "Sea of Reeds") evidently referred originally to (1) a series of lakes and marshes between the head of the Gulf of Suez and the Mediterranean, the region generally regarded as the site of the events described in Exodus 14, and was extended to include (2) the Gulf of Suez, and (3) the Gulf of Aqaba.

11.6   Dathan and Abiram: see Num 16.1-34.

11.29 Mount Gerizim...Mount Ebal: see Josh 8.30-35.

12.3   Asherah: see 7.5.

12.6   Tithes: see 14.22-29.

13.1   Dreams: regarded as a means whereby God revealed his will.

14.12-18   Cormorants: the identification of some of the birds in verses 12-18 is uncertain.

14.21 In its mother's milk: a method used by Canaanites in their fertility rites.

(25)

15.12   sells himself; or is sold.

15.18   at half the cost of a hired servant; or and has worked twice as hard as a hired servant.

16.1   Abib: the first Jewish month (later called Nisan), which began with the first new moon occurring after the modern March 11.

16.10   Then: about the eighth day of Sivan, the third Jewish month, which began with the first new moon occurring after the modern May 9.

16.13   Festival of Shelters: beginning the fifteenth day of Tishri, the seventh Jewish month, which began with the first new moon occurring after the modern September 4.

16.21   Asherah: see 7.5.

17.16   to buy horses; or in exchange for horses.

18.8   Probable text and he may keep whatever his family sends him; Hebrew unclear.

18.15   a prophet...him; or prophets...them.

18.18   a prophet...him...he; or prophets...them...they.

18.19   He will speak in my name, and I; or When a prophet speaks in my name, I.

19.2-3   The territory: Canaan, west of the Jordan; three cities of refuge in the land east of the Jordan have already been provided for (see 4.41-43).

19.9   Three more: either the three east of the Jordan (see 4.41-43) or three additional cities in territory to the north and northeast.

20.6   Harvest its grapes: this would ordinarily take place five years after planting the vineyard (see Lev 19.23-25).

21.12   shave her head; or trim her hair.

22.8   The roof: it was flat and was used as a place where people would rest after the day's work.

22.12   Tassels: ornaments made of threads or cords bound at one end.

23.4   Balaam: see Num 22.1--24.25.

23.7   Your relatives: the Edomites were descendants of Esau, brother of Jacob, who was the ancestor of the Israelites.

23.15   If a slave runs away: it seems that this law applies to a slave from another country (see "any of your towns" in verse 16).

23.17   Temple prostitute: such a person was found in Canaanite temples, where fertility gods were worshiped. It was believed that intercourse with such a prostitute assured fertile fields and herds.

24.1   something about her that he doesn't like; or that she is guilty of some shameful conduct.

24.5   make his wife happy; or be happy with his wife.

24.8   Dreaded skin disease: traditionally thought of as leprosy; the Hebrew word, however, included other skin diseases as well.

24.9   Miriam: see Num 12.9-10.

25.17   The Amalekites: see Exo 17.8-14.

26.2   Harvest: a reference to the Harvest Festival (see 16.9-12).

26.5   My ancestor: Jacob.

26.14   for the dead; or to the dead.

26.19   bring praise and honor to his name; or receive praise and honor.

27.4   Mount Ebal: in the hill country of Israel, some 44 kilometers north of Jerusalem, near the city of Shechem.

27.7   Fellowship offerings: sacrifices in which only part of the animal was burned on the altar; the rest was eaten by the worshipers.

27.12   Mount Gerizim: south of Mount Ebal (verse 4), across Schechem Valley.

27.15   Amen: a Hebrew word meaning "it is so" or "so be it."

28.48   The LORD; or Your enemies.

28.68   he; or I.

29.1   Moab: see 1.5.

29.23   Sodom and Gomorrah: see Gen 19.24-25.

30.16   One ancient translation If you obey the commands of the LORD your God; Hebrew does not have these words.

31.9   Covenant Box: see Exo 25.10-22.

31.10   The year that debts are canceled: see 15.1-11.
        Festival of Shelters: see 16.13-17.

32.5   Probable text But you...people; Hebrew unclear.

(27)

32.8   A heavenly being: a guardian angel or a god.

32.11   teaching its young to fly; or watching over its young.

32.22   The world below: a reference to the world of the dead (see Num 16.30).

32.50   Aaron died: see Num 20.22-29.

32.51   Meribah: see Exo 17.1-7; Num 20.1-13.

33.2   Mount Paran: in the wilderness of Paran (see Num 10.12), south-west of Edom.
        Probable text Ten thousand...right hand; Hebrew unclear.

33.3   One ancient translation his people; Hebrew the peoples.
        Probable text bow at; Hebrew unclear.

33.7   Probable text Fight for...enemies; Hebrew The tribe of Judah will fight for itself, and the LORD will help it against its enemies.

33.8   Urim and Thummim: two objects used by the priest to determine God's will; it is not known precisely how they were used.
        Massah...Meribah: see Exo 17.1-7; Num 20.1-13.

33.12   And he dwells in their midst; or They live under his protection.

33.16   Spoke from the burning bush: see Exo 3.1-6.

33.18   The sea: the Mediterranean.

33.21   One ancient translation when the leaders of Israel were gathered together; Hebrew unclear.

33.22   Bashan: a region northeast of Lake Galilee.

34.1   Mount Pisgah: see 3.27.
        Gilead: on the east side of the Jordan River.

34.3   Zoar: at the southeastern end of the Dead Sea.

JOSHUA

1.2   Cross the Jordan River: the Israelites are in the territory of Moab, on the east side of the Jordan (see Num 33.50-51).

1.4   Your borders: see also Deut 11.24.
        The Hittite country: land in northern Syria that had once been part of the Hittite empire.

1.8   The book of the Law: probably a reference to what is now part if not all of the book of Deuteronomy.

1.12   Half the tribe of Manasseh: the half that settled in the territory east of the Jordan (see Num 32.33; Deut 3.13); the other half occupied territory in Canaan, on the west side of the Jordan (see 22.6-8).

1.13   Moses told you: see Num 32.28-33; Deut 3.18-20.

2.1   The camp at Acacia: northeast of the Dead Sea (see Num 33.49). Jericho: the most important city in the region, some 18 kilometers west of the Jordan.

2.4-6   Flax: a plant from whose stem a fiber was made; the fact that the stalks had been placed on the roof, presumably to dry out, may indicate that it was spring (see 3.14-15).

2.10   The Red Sea: (in Hebrew literally "Sea of Reeds") evidently referred originally to (1) a series of lakes and marshes between the head of the Gulf of Suez and the Mediterranean, the region generally regarded as the site of the events described in Exodus 14, and was extended to include (2) the Gulf of Suez, and (3) the Gulf of Aqaba.

2.14   May God...say; or We will protect you if you protect us.

2.23   Crossed the river: back to the east side, where the Israelites were camped (see 1.2).

3.3   The Covenant Box: a wooden chest covered with gold, in which were kept the two stone tablets on which were inscribed the Ten Commandments (see Exo 37.1-9).

3.5   Purify yourselves: a ritual to remove any ceremonial impurity which prevented the proper performance of religious duties.

3.14-15   Harvest time: in the spring.

3.16   Adam: some 30 kilometers north of Jericho; Zarethan: a city some 20 kilometers farther north.

4.9   Are still there: at the time of the writing of the account.

4.12   Reuben and Gad and...half the tribe of Manasseh: see 1.12-15.

4.19   First month: Abib (or Nisan), the Jewish month that began with the first new moon occurring after the modern March 11. Gilgal: about 4 kilometers northeast of Jericho.

5.2   Circumcise: to cut off the foreskin of the penis, as a sign of God's covenant with his people (see Gen 17.9-14).

5.3   Called: that is, the name (literally "hill of foreskins") was given after the mass circumcision of the male Hebrews.

5.9   Gilgal: this name sounds like the Hebrew for "removed."

5.10   Passover: see Exo 12.1-14.
The month: Abib (see 4.19).

5.12   The manna: see Exo 16.1-35.

6.17   An offering to the LORD: what was thus dedicated to God had to
be totally destroyed; nothing could be kept as personal loot (see
Lev 27.28-29; Num 21.2).

6.23   Rahab: she eventually married Salmon (Matt 1.5) and thus became
the great-great-grandmother of King David (see Ruth 4.18-22).

6.25   This day: the time of the writing of the account.

6.26   The LORD's curse: see the fulfillment of this curse in 1 Kgs 16.34.

7.2   Ai: a city some 24 kilometers west of Jericho; Bethel was about
3 kilometers northwest of Ai.

7.14   Pick out: by means of drawing lots, a way of determining God's
will (see 14.2; Deut 33.8).

8.15   The barren country: to the east of Ai.

8.17   One ancient translation Ai; Hebrew Ai and Bethel.

8.28   Today: see 6.25.

8.30   Mount Ebal: some 32 kilometers north of Ai.

8.31   As it says in the Law of Moses: see Exo 20.25; Deut 27.5-6.
Fellowship offerings: a sacrifice in which only part of the
animal was burned on the altar; the rest was eaten by the worshipers.

8.32   the stones; or stones.

8.33   Covenant Box: see 3.3.
Mount Gerizim: south of Mount Ebal, across Shechem Valley.
Moses had commanded: see Deut 27.11-13.

9.3   Gibeon: about 11 kilometers southwest of Ai.

9.6   Gilgal: see 4.19.

9.7   Maybe you live nearby: according to the Mosaic law, Israel could
make a peace treaty only with people who lived at a great distance
(see Deut 20.10-15).

9.10   King Sihon...King Og: see Num 21.21-35.

9.14   Accepted some food: a way of sealing the treaty.

9.27   This day: the time of the writing of the account.
The place: the Temple in Jerusalem.

10.1   Jerusalem: at that time it was a Jebusite city.

10.3   Hebron: a city some 32 kilometers southwest of Jerusalem; Jarmuth,
Lachish, and Eglon were cities 25 to 55 kilometers southwest of
Jerusalem.

10.9   From Gilgal to Gibeon: a distance of about 32 kilometers.

10.12   Aijalon Valley: about 15 kilometers west of Gibeon.

10.13   The Book of Jashar: a book, no longer in existence, of Hebrew
poetry (see also 2 Sam 1.18).

10.16   Makkedah: some 30 kilometers southwest of Gibeon.

10.29-39   Libnah...Lachish...Eglon...Hebron...Debir: cities in the
southern part of Palestine.

11.1   Hazor: a city some 15 kilometers north of Lake Galilee; this
section (11.1-15) describes Joshua's victories in northern
Palestine.

11.5   Merom Brook: a stream that flows into the northwest corner of
Lake Galilee.

11.22   Gaza, Gath, and Ashdod: Philistine cities, near the Mediterranean
coast.

12.2   Sihon: see Num 21.21-30; Deut 2.26-37.
Probable text (see 13.16; Deut 2.36) the city in; Hebrew does not
have these words.

12.4   King Og: see Num 21.33-35; Deut 3.1-10.
The Rephaim: a race of giants who lived in Canaan (see Deut 2.10-
11; 3.11).

12.23   One ancient translation Galilee; Hebrew Gilgal.

13.9   Their territory: see Deut 3.12-17.

13.12   The Rephaim: see 12.4.

13.14   The LORD had told Moses: see Deut 18.1-2.

13.22   Balaam: see Num 22.1--24.25.

13.33   Tribe of Levi: see 13.14.

14.1   Eleazar: son of Aaron, who succeeded his father as high priest
(see Num 20.22-28).

(31)

14.2   Drawing lots: this was usually done by using especially marked stones to determine God's will (see also Deut 33.8).

14.3-4 The Levites: see 13.14.

14.6   The LORD said: see Num 14.30.
        Caleb: one of the twelve men sent by Moses to spy out the land of Canaan (see Num 13).

14.12   The LORD promised me: see Num 14.24-25.

14.13   Hebron: see 10.3.

14.15   Debir: a city some 16 kilometers southwest of Hebron.

15.18   Probable text (see Judges 1.14) Othniel urged her; Hebrew she urged Othniel.

15.63   Still live there: at the time of the writing of the account.

16.1   The descendants of Joseph: the people descended from Ephraim and Manasseh, the two sons of Joseph (see 14.3-4).

16.10   This day: the time of the writing of the account.

17.11   Probable text Dor (the one on the coast); Hebrew unclear.

17.18   Iron chariots: chariots equipped with iron armor plates.

18.1   Shiloh: a town some 32 kilometers north of Jerusalem, which became the religious center of the Israelites.
        The Tent of the LORD's presence: the place of worship, where God met his people (see Exo 26); it was used until Solomon built the Temple in Jerusalem.

18.6   Draw lots: see 14.2.

18.15   Probable text and went; Hebrew and went westward.

19.34   One ancient translation the Jordan; Hebrew Judah at the Jordan.

19.51   Eleazar the priest: see 14.1.
        Drawing lots: see 14.2.
        The Tent of the LORD's presence: see 18.1.

20.2   I had Moses tell you: see Num 35.9-34; Deut 19.1-13.

21.2   The LORD had commanded through Moses: see Num 35.1-8.

21.4   Aaron: grandson of Kohath (see Exo 6.18,20).

21.4-7 Kohath, Gershon, Merari: the three sons of Levi (see Exo 6.16).

21.8 Drawing lots: see 14.2.

22.10 still on the west side; or on the east side.

22.17 Our sin at Peor: see Num 25.1-9.

22.20 Achan: see 7.1-26.

23.6 The book of the Law of Moses: see 1.8.

24.1 Shechem: a city in the highlands of Israel, some 50 kilometers north of Jerusalem.

24.6 Red Sea: see 2.10.

24.9 Balak...Balaam: see Num 22.1--24.25.

24.12 The two Amorite kings: Sihon and Og (see Num 21.21-35).

24.25 for; or with.

24.30 His own land: see 19.49-50.

24.32 The body of Joseph: see Gen 50.24-26; Exo 13.19.
Land that Jacob had bought: see Gen 33.19.

JUDGES

1.1 Joshua's death: see Josh 24.29-30.
Asked the LORD: probably by means of drawing lots (see Josh 14.2).

1.4 Bezek: location unknown.

1.7 Picked up scraps under my table: a sign of defeat and humiliation.

1.10 Hebron: a city some 32 kilometers south of Jerusalem (see Josh 10.36-37).

1.14 Some ancient translations Othniel urged her; Hebrew she urged Othniel.

1.16 Moses' father-in-law: see Exo 2.16-21.
Some ancient translations Amalekites; Hebrew people.

1.17 Hormah: this name in Hebrew means "destruction."

1.18-19 One ancient translation But they did not capture; Hebrew And they captured.
Gaza, Ashkelon, or Ekron: three of the five Philistine cities (see Josh 13.3).
Iron chariots: chariots equipped with iron armor plates.

1.20 Moses had commanded: see Josh 15.13-14.

1.22-23   Bethel: a city some 19 kilometers north of Jerusalem.

1.36   One ancient translation Edomite; Hebrew Amorite.

2.1   Gilgal: see Josh 4.19.
Bochim: this place has not been identified; perhaps it stands here for Bethel (see 1.22-23).

2.3   Some ancient translations enemies; Hebrew sides.

2.5   Bochim: this name in Hebrew means "those who cry."

2.11   The Baals: the male gods of fertility worshiped by the Canaanites.

2.13   The Astartes: the female gods of fertility and war worshiped by the Canaanites.

3.3   Five Philistine cities: see Josh 13.3.

3.7   Baal and Asherah: the male and the female fertility gods of the Canaanites.

3.12   Moab: a country on the east side of the Dead Sea.

3.22   Probable text it stuck...legs; Hebrew unclear.

4.2   Hazor: see Josh 11.1.

4.3   Iron chariots: see 1.18-19.

4.6   Mount Tabor: in Galilee, some 19 kilometers west of the southern end of Lake Galilee.

4.18   hid him behind a curtain; or covered him with a rug.

5.7   abandoned, Deborah...you came; or abandoned; they stood empty until I, Deborah, came.

5.10   Tell of; or Think about.

5.11   from their cities; or to their gates.

5.13   One ancient translation him; Hebrew me.

5.14   Probable text They came; Hebrew Their root.
One ancient translation into the valley; Hebrew in Amalek.

5.28   Some ancient translations gazed; Hebrew cried out.

5.30   Probable text queen; Hebrew plunder.

6.1   People of Midian: a nomadic people who roamed the desert regions southeast of Palestine.

6.25   bull and another bull seven years old; or bull, the seven-year-
old one.
Baal...Asherah: see 3.7.
The symbol: a wooden pole.

6.26   the second bull; or the bull.

6.32   Jerubbaal: this name in Hebrew means "Let Baal defend himself."

8.4   Crossed it: to the east side of the river.

8.31   Concubine: a female servant who, although not a wife, had
sexual relations with her master. She had important legal rights,
and her master was referred to as her husband.

8.33   The Baals: see 2.11.

9.6   Shechem: a city in the highlands of Israel, some 50 kilometers
north of Jerusalem.

9.29   One ancient translation I would tell; Hebrew He told.

9.31   Probable text Arumah; Hebrew unclear.

9.45   Covered the ground with salt: in order to destroy its fertility.

10.4   Rode thirty donkeys: a sign of wealth and importance.

10.6   The Baals and the Astartes: see 2.11,13.

10.17   Gilead: on the east side of the Jordan, north of the Dead Sea.

11.16   Kadesh: also known as Kadesh Barnea, an oasis some 145 kilometers
northwest of the northern end of the Gulf of Aqaba (see Num 20.1,
14-21).

11.24   Chemosh: usually identified as the god of the Moabites; the chief
god of the Ammonites was Molech (see 1 Kgs 11.7).

11.37   Grieve: it was a tragedy for an Israelite woman to die unmarried
and childless.

12.6   Shibboleth: the Ephraimites could not easily pronounce the "sh"
sound; the word itself means "ear of grain."

12.7   One ancient translation his hometown; Hebrew the towns.

12.8   Bethlehem: not the better known town south of Jerusalem, but a
town some 11 kilometers northwest of Nazareth, in the territory of
the tribe of Zebulun (Josh 19.15).

12.14   Donkeys: see 10.4.

13.2   Tribe of Dan: at this time it was located in the southwest, near the coastal plains occupied by the Philistines; later it moved north (see chapter 18).

13.5   Nazirite: a person who showed his devotion to God by taking vows not to drink wine or beer or cut his hair or touch corpses (see Num 6.1-8).

13.6   the angel; or an angel.

13.18   name of wonder; or mysterious name.

13.19   Some ancient translations who works wonders; Hebrew and working wonders while Manoah and his wife watched.

14.15   Some ancient translations fourth; Hebrew seventh.
        set fire...you with it; or burn you and your family.

14.18   Probable text bedroom; Hebrew sun.

14.19   Ashkelon: one of the five Philistine cities (see 1.18-19).

15.6   burned the woman...house; or burned the woman and her family to death.

15.16   Piles: this word sounds like the Hebrew for "donkey."

15.17   Ramath Lehi: this name in Hebrew means "Jawbone Hill."

15.19   Hakkore: this name in Hebrew means "caller."

16.3   Hebron: some 65 kilometers east of Gaza.

16.5   Five: there were five Philistine cities (see Josh 13.3).

16.13   Loom: a device used for weaving cloth from thread or yarn.

16.13-14 One ancient translation and make it tight (in verse 13)...into the loom (in verse 14); Hebrew does not have these words.

16.17   Nazirite: see 13.5.

16.19   Probable text who cut off; Hebrew and she cut off.

16.24-25 make him entertain us; or make fun of him.
        made him entertain them; or made fun of him.

16.27   entertain them; or and making fun of him.

17.5   Ephod: either an object to be worshiped or to be used in divination; see also Exo 25.7.

17.7   Bethlehem: a town some 8 kilometers south of Jerusalem.

17.10   Probable text your food; Hebrew your food. So the Levite went.

18.2   qualified; or brave.

18.7   Sidonians: residents of Sidon, a Phoenician city on the Mediterranean coast, north of Palestine.
Probable text They were...needed; Hebrew unclear.

18.14   Ephod: see 17.5.

18.30   Moses; or Manasseh.
Exile: to Assyria, about 733 B.C.

18.31   The Tent: the place of worship, where God met his people (see
Exo 26); it was used until Solomon built the Temple in Jerusalem.
Shiloh: a town some 32 kilometers north of Jerusalem, which
became the religious center of the Israelites.

19.1   Concubine: see 8.31.

19.14   Gibeah: about 8 kilometers north of Jerusalem.

19.18   One ancient translation home; Hebrew to the house of the LORD.

20.1   Mizpah: about 12 kilometers north of Jerusalem.

20.9   One ancient translation to attack Gibeah; Hebrew to Gibeah.

20.10   One ancient translation Gibeah; Hebrew Geba.

20.15-16   Some ancient translations men; Hebrew men. In all this number
there were seven hundred specially chosen men.

20.18   Bethel: see 1.22-23.

20.22-23   Asked him: see 1.1.

20.27-28   Covenant Box: a wooden chest covered with gold, in which were
kept the two stone tablets on which were inscribed the Ten Commandments (see Exo 37.1-9).

20.33   One ancient translation the city (that is, Gibeah); Hebrew Geba.

20.42   Probable text city; Hebrew cities.

20.43   Verse 43 in Hebrew is unclear.

21.4   Fellowship sacrifices: a sacrifice in which only part of the
animal was burned on the altar; the rest was eaten by the worshipers.

21.21   The feast: commemorating the grape harvest.

(37)

21.22   One ancient translation you; Hebrew us.
        Probable text you; Hebrew we.

RUTH

1.1-2   Before Israel had a king: in the days when Israel was ruled by
        leaders called judges.
        Clan: a subdivision of a tribe.
        Bethlehem: a town about 8 kilometers south of Jerusalem.
        Moab: on the east side of the Dead Sea.

1.4   Orpah: Chilion's wife; Ruth was Mahlon's wife (see 4.10).

1.11   Have sons again for you to marry: a reference to the Hebrew law
        which required a man to marry his dead brother's wife (see Deut
        25.5-10).

1.13   sorry for you; or bitter about what has happened to you.

1.14   One ancient translation and went back home; Hebrew does not have
        these words.

1.15   god; or gods.
        God: Chemosh was the god of the Moabites (see 1 Kgs 11.33).

1.17   anything but death; or even death.

1.20   Naomi...Marah: in Hebrew Naomi means "pleasant" and Marah means
        "bitter."

1.22   Barley harvest: in late April or early May.

2.1   family; or clan (see 1.2).

2.2   Gather the grain that the harvest workers leave: this was permit-
        ted by Hebrew law (see Lev 19.9-10; Deut 24.19).

2.13   You are very kind; or Please be kind.

2.20   The dead: Naomi is thinking of her dead husband and sons.

2.23   All the barley and wheat had been harvested: toward the end of
        June.

3.2   Evening: late in the day there was usually a wind which would
        blow away the chaff as the worker threw the mixture of grain and
        chaff into the air with a wooden shovel.

3.4   Where he lies down; he would spend the night at the threshing
        place in order to guard the grain.

3.15   she returned to town with it; some Hebrew manuscripts have he
        returned to town.

4.1   The man whom Boaz had mentioned: in his conversation with Ruth (see 3.12).

4.5   Some ancient translations from Naomi; then you are also buying Ruth; Hebrew from Naomi and from Ruth.
The dead man: Elimelech, to whom the field belonged (verse 3); any child born to Ruth would be considered Elimelech's (and Mahlon's) descendant and would inherit the field.

4.8   One ancient translation gave it to Boaz; Hebrew does not have these words.

4.11   Rachel and Leah: see Gen 35.23-26.

4.12   Perez: ancestor of Boaz; and see Gen 38.1-30.

4.16   held him close; or adopted him.

1 SAMUEL

1.3   Almighty: this title for God, which appears here for the first time in the Old Testament, refers to him as the commander of Israel's armies (see 17.45) or of the heavenly powers.
Shiloh: a town some 32 kilometers north of Jerusalem, which became the religious center of the Israelites.

1.5   And even...because; or To Hannah, however, he would give a special share, because he loved her very much, even though.

1.11   Never have his hair cut: a sign of dedication to the LORD (see Num 6.5).

1.20   Samuel: this name, which in Hebrew means "name of God," is here related to the Hebrew verb for "ask."

1.22   Is weaned: at that time this usually happened when the child was two years old.

1.23   Some ancient translations your; Hebrew his.

1.24   Some ancient translations a three-year-old bull; Hebrew three bulls.

1.28   Some ancient translations they; Hebrew he.

2.6   World of the dead: called Sheol and thought of as a vast abyss in the depths of the earth.

2.8   The foundations of the earth: it was believed that beneath the seas there was a foundation, upon which the earth rested.

(39)

2.22   Tent of the LORD's presence: the place of worship, where God met his people (see Exo 26); it was used until Solomon built the Temple in Jerusalem.

2.28   Ephod: a vest-like garment worn by the High Priest (see Exo 28.4-12), to which was attached a breastpiece in which were kept the Urim and Thummim, two objects used in determining God's will (see Exo 28.15-30).

2.29   One ancient translation look with greed; Hebrew unclear.

2.32   Probable text look with envy; Hebrew unclear.

2.33   One of your descendants: Abiathar, who escaped death when all the other priests at Nob were killed (see 22.8-13; 1 Kgs 2.26-27). One ancient translation he; Hebrew you.

3.3   Covenant Box: a wooden chest covered with gold, in which were kept the two stone tablets on which were inscribed the Ten Commandments (see Exo 37.1-9).
        The lamp: it was kept burning all night (see Exo 27.20-21).

3.13   One ancient translation I have already told him; Hebrew I will tell him.

4.1   At that time: the date is around 1050 B.C.
        One ancient translation the Philistines...so; Hebrew does not have these words.
        Ebenezer...Aphek: two localities in the northeastern section of the area controlled by the Philistines, on the border with Israelite territory.

4.3   Covenant Box: see 3.3.
        he; or it.

4.4   Almighty: see 1.3.
        Winged creatures: figures which symbolized God's majesty and were associated with his presence with his people; see a description of them in Exo 25.18-20.

4.8   Those powerful gods: the Philistines mistakenly thought that, like themselves, the Hebrews worshiped several gods.

4.12   All the way: a distance of some 37 kilometers.

4.21   Ichabod: this name in Hebrew means "no glory."

5.1   Ashdod: one of the five Philistine cities (see 6.17).

5.5   Today: the time of the writing of the account.

5.6   Tumors: the association of tumors with an abundance of mice suggests that this was a case of bubonic plague (see 6.5).

6.9   Beth Shemesh: an Israelite town about 20 kilometers east of the Philistine border.

6.21   Kiriath Jearim: about 11 kilometers from Beth Shemesh and about 15 kilometers northwest of Jerusalem.

7.3   Astarte: the female god of fertility and war worshiped by the Canaanites.

7.4   Baal: the male god of fertility worshiped by the Canaanites.

7.5   Mizpah: about 8 kilometers northwest of Jerusalem.

8.2   Beersheba: in the southern part of the territory of Judah.

8.16   One ancient translation cattle; Hebrew young men.

9.20   who is it...much?; or who is to have the most desirable thing in Israel?

9.24   Some ancient translations Samuel; Hebrew He (that is, the cook). Probable text I saved it...invited; Hebrew unclear.

9.25   One ancient translation they fixed up a bed for Saul; Hebrew he spoke with Saul.
        On the roof: at that time houses had flat roofs, and it was common for people to sleep on them.

9.26   Some ancient translations and he slept there; Hebrew and they got up early.

10.1   Anoints: the action of pouring olive oil on someone's head as a sign that God had chosen that person for some special office.
        Some ancient translations as ruler of his people...the LORD has chosen you; Hebrew does not have these words.

10.5   camp; or pillar, or governor.

10.17   Mizpah: see 7.5.

10.20   Picked: God's will was probably revealed by the drawing of lots (see Josh 14.2).

10.21   One ancient translation Then the men of the family of Matri came forward; Hebrew does not have these words.

10.26   One ancient translation Some powerful men; Hebrew The army.

11.1   Ammon: on the east side of the Jordan River.
        Jabesh: an Israelite town on the east side of the Jordan.

11.8   Bezek: on the west side of the Jordan River.

11.15   Fellowship sacrifices: sacrifices in which only part of the animal was burned on the altar; the rest was eaten by the worshipers.

12.7   One ancient translation by reminding you; Hebrew does not have these words.

12.8   One ancient translation and the Egyptians oppressed them; Hebrew does not have these words.

12.10   Baal and Astarte: see 7.3,4.

12.11   Some ancient translations Barak; Hebrew Bedan.

12.15   One ancient translation your king; Hebrew your ancestors.

12.21   Some ancient translations after; Hebrew because after.

13.1   One ancient translation does not have verse 1; Hebrew has as verse 1 Saul was...years old when he became king, and he was king of Israel for two years. The Hebrew text is defective at two points in this verse.

13.3   killed the Philistine commander; or defeated the Philistines camping.
        Geba: some 8 kilometers northeast of Gibeah.

13.5   Bethaven: probably another name for Bethel, the Israelite religious center some 19 kilometers north of Jerusalem.

13.7   Crossed the Jordan River: to the east side.

13.8   As Samuel had instructed: see 10.8.

13.15   Some ancient translations on his way...went from Gilgal; Hebrew does not have these words.

13.20   One ancient translation sickles; Hebrew plows.

13.21   Probable text the charge...fixing goads; Hebrew unclear.

14.3   wearing; or carrying.
        Ephod: see 2.28.

14.7   One ancient translation you want to do; Hebrew you want to do. Turn.

14.12   tell; or show.

14.14   Probable text in an area of about half an acre; Hebrew unclear.

14.18   One ancient translation ephod (see 2.28); Hebrew Covenant Box.
        One ancient translation On that day...Israel; Hebrew Because on that day God's Covenant Box and the people of Israel.

14.21   Some ancient translations changed sides again; Hebrew around also.

14.23   Bethaven: see 13.5.

14.24   A curse on anyone who eats any food today: to abstain from eating was regarded as a means of winning God's help in battle.

14.25   Probable text They all; Hebrew All the land.

14.33   Eating meat with the blood in it: see Lev 17.10-12.
A big stone: to be used as an altar.
One ancient translation here; Hebrew today.

14.36   Consult: by means of the sacred stones carried in the ephod (see verse 41).

14.41   Some ancient translations answer me by the sacred stones...your people Israel; Hebrew does not have these words.
Urim...Thummim: two stones used by the priest to determine God's will; it is not known precisely how they were used.

14.47   One ancient translation was victorious; Hebrew acted wickedly.

15.1   Almighty: see 1.3.

15.2   Amalek: a territory southwest of Palestine.
Opposed the Israelites: see Exo 17.8-14; Deut 25.17-19.

15.9   One ancient translation the best calves and lambs; Hebrew unclear.
Some ancient translations useless or worthless; Hebrew unclear.

15.12   Carmel: a town some 11 kilometers south of Hebron.

15.15   Destroyed completely: these animals had been unconditionally dedicated to God and had to be destroyed (see Lev 27.28).

15.32   trembling with fear...die; or confidently, thinking to himself, "Surely the bitter danger of death is past!"

16.4   Seer: see 9.9-11.

16.5   Purify yourselves: a ritual to remove any ceremonial impurity which prevented the proper performance of religious duties.

17.4   Hebrew over nine feet; one ancient Hebrew manuscript and one ancient translation over six feet.

17.7   Loom: a device used for weaving cloth from thread or yarn.

17.12   Some ancient translations a very old man; Hebrew unclear.

17.25   to pay taxes; or either to pay taxes or serve him.

17.52   One ancient translation Gath; Hebrew a valley.

18.7   Tambourine: a small drum with pieces of metal in the rim, held
in one hand and shaken.
Lyre: a stringed instrument like a harp.

18.25   Payment for the bride: it was the custom of the time for a man
to pay a certain sum to the father of the girl he intended to marry.
Foreskins: the Philistines, unlike the Hebrews, did not practice
circumcision.

19.1   that he planned to kill; or to kill.

19.18,19   Naioth; or the huts (where prophets lived; see verse 20).

19.20   Some ancient translations They saw; Hebrew He saw.

19.22,23   Naioth: see verse 18.

19.24   Has even Saul become a prophet?: see 10.11-12 for another
account of the origin of this saying.

20.1   Naioth: see 19.18.

20.3   One ancient translation answered; Hebrew made a vow again.

20.5   To eat: a religious meal celebrating the New Moon Festival, when
all members of the household were supposed to be present.

20.12   One ancient translation be our witness; Hebrew does not have
these words.

20.14   Some ancient translations if I die; Hebrew that I may not die.

20.16   Verses 15-16 in Hebrew are unclear.

20.19   Some ancient translations your absence will be noticed; Hebrew
go down.
Probable text the pile of stones there; Hebrew the Ezel Stone.

20.25   One ancient translation sat across the table from him; Hebrew
stood up.

20.41   Probable text the pile of stones; Hebrew the south.
Probable text David's grief was even greater than Jonathan's;
Hebrew unclear.

21.1   Nob: a town some 4 kilometers east of Jerusalem.

21.4   Sacred bread: the loaves offered to God (see verse 6 and
Lev 24.5-9); only the priests were allowed to eat this bread.
Sexual relations: this would make a man ritually impure for a
time and prevent him from taking part in any religious ceremony
(see Lev 15.16-18).

21.9   Ephod:either an object to be worshiped or to be used in divination; see also 2.28.

21.10   Gath: one of the five Philistine cities, near the Mediterranean coast.

21.13   city; or palace.

22.1   Adullam: some 24 kilometers southwest of Jerusalem.

22.3   Moab: on the east side of the Dead Sea.

22.5   Hereth: location unknown.

22.6   Gibeah: some 8 kilometers north of Jerusalem.

22.9   Doeg: see 21.7.

22.10   Asked the LORD: see 14.36.

22.14   Some ancient translations captain of; Hebrew he turned to.

22.15   Yes, I consulted...time; or Now, have I done something wrong by consulting God for him? Not at all!

22.18   Ephod: see 2.28.

22.22   Some ancient translations I am responsible; Hebrew I have turned.

23.1   Keilah: southwest of Adullam (see 22.1).

23.2   Asked the LORD: see 14.36.

23.6   Ephod: see 2.28.

23.14   Ziph: a desolate area some 16 kilometers southeast of Hebron.

23.24   Maon: a short distance south of Ziph (verse 14).

23.29   Engedi: some 25 kilometers east of Ziph, near the west shore of the Dead Sea.

25.1   Paran: far to the south, in the Sinai Peninsula; one ancient translation has Maon (see 23.24).

25.2-3 Carmel: see 15.12.

25.22   One ancient translation me; Hebrew my enemies.

25.25   A fool: this is the meaning of the Hebrew name Nabal.

25.28   you will not do anything evil; or no evil will happen to you.

26.6   Zeruiah: according to 1 Chr 2.16 she was David's sister; her sons Abishai and Joab were his nephews.

26.19   Worship foreign gods: at that time it was believed that a god's sovereignty extended only over the land that was his; so in a foreign country David would not be able to worship the God of Israel.

27.2   Gath: see 21.10.

28.4   Mount Gilboa: some 32 kilometers southwest of Lake Galilee.

28.6   Urim and Thummim: see 14.41.

28.7   Endor: about 16 kilometers north of Mount Gilboa.

28.9   he forced...Israel; or he put to death the fortunetellers and mediums in Israel.

28.13   Coming up from the earth: from Sheol, the world of the dead (see 2.6).

28.19   Will join me: in the world of the dead.

29.1   Aphek: see 4.1.

29.11   Jezreel: some 120 kilometers from Aphek.

30.7   Abiathar: see 23.6.
        Ephod: see 2.28.

30.8   Asked the LORD: see 14.36.

30.20   Probable text his men...front of them; Hebrew unclear.

31.1   Mount Gilboa: see 28.4.

31.7   Jezreel Valley: to the north and east of Mount Gilboa.

31.10   Astarte: see 7.3.

31.11   Jabesh in Gilead: see chapter 11.

2 SAMUEL

1.18   One ancient translation it; Hebrew the bow.
        The Book of Jashar: see Josh 10.13 for another reference to this book, which no longer exists.

1.20   Gath...Ashkelon: two of the five Philistine cities (see 1 Sam 6.17).

1.21   Shield: made of tough leather, not metal; the oil would keep it
in good condition.

2.1   Asked the LORD: see 1 Sam 14.36.
Hebron: some 32 kilometers southwest of Jerusalem.

2.8   Abner: cousin of Saul (see 1 Sam 14.50-51).
Mahanaim: in Gilead, on the east side of the Jordan River.

2.9   One ancient translation Asher; Hebrew Assyria.

2.12   Gibeon: some 10 kilometers northwest of Jerusalem.

2.18   Zeruiah: see 1 Sam 26.6.

2.23   Probable text with a backward thrust; Hebrew unclear.

3.7   Saul's concubine: a royal concubine became the property of the
next king; the accusation against Abner was that he was acting as
though he were the king.

3.12   One ancient translation at Hebron; Hebrew where he (Abner) was.

3.14   Michal: Saul's daughter, and so a help in David's claim to be
Saul's successor.

3.19   Benjamin: the tribe of which Saul had been a member.

4.6   Verse 6 follows one ancient translation; Hebrew They went on
into the house carrying wheat, and struck him in the belly. Then
Rechab and his brother Baanah escaped.

5.7   Zion: the name of the hill on which the Jebusite fortress was
located.

5.8   Verse 8 in Hebrew is unclear.

5.10   Almighty: see 1 Sam 1.3.

5.11   Tyre: a Phoenician city on the Mediterranean, north of Palestine.

5.18   Rephaim Valley: probably southwest of Jerusalem.

5.19   Asked the LORD: see 1 Sam 14.36.

5.20   Baal Perazim: this name in Hebrew means "Lord of the Breakthrough."

6.2   Probable text (see 1 Chr 13.6) to Baalah; Hebrew from Baaley, or
from the leaders.
Covenant Box: see 1 Sam 3.3.
Winged creatures: figures which symbolized God's majesty and were
associated with his presence with his people; see a description of
them in Exo 25.18-20.

6.3   Abinadab's home: see 1 Sam 7.1-2.

6.3,4   Ahio; or his brother.

6.5   One ancient translation (and see 1 Chr 13.8) and singing with all their might; Hebrew with all the fir trees.

6.7   Probable text his irreverence; Hebrew unclear.

6.8   Perez Uzzah: this name in Hebrew means "Punishment of Uzzah."

6.17   Fellowship offerings: see 1 Sam 11.15.

6.19   a piece of roasted meat; or a cake of dates.

6.22   One ancient translation You; Hebrew I.

7.2   Covenant Box: see 1 Sam 3.3.

7.7   Probable text (see 1 Chr 17.6) leaders; Hebrew tribes.

7.8   Almighty: see 1 Sam 1.3.

7.18   Tent of the LORD's presence: see 1 Sam 2.22.

7.19   Probable text you let a man see this; Hebrew this is a law for men.

7.23   Probable text them; Hebrew you (plural).
        One ancient translation (and see 1 Chr 17.21) You drove out; Hebrew for your land.

8.1   Probable text over the land; Hebrew unclear.

8.3   Zobah: a region north of Damascus.

8.6   set up military camps in; or placed military commanders over.

8.9   Hamath: a region north of Zobah (verse 3).

8.14   set up military camps; or placed military commanders.
        Edom: the country south of the Dead Sea; the Edomites were descendants of Esau.

8.18   Some ancient translations was in charge of; Hebrew does not have these words.

9.3   Crippled: see 4.4.

9.11   One ancient translation the king's; Hebrew my.

10.1   King Nahash: see 1 Sam 11.1-11.
        Ammon: a land on the east side of the Dead Sea.

11.1   Rabbah: the capital of Ammon (see 10.1).

11.2   Walked around: in those days the roof was flat and was used as a place for rest and leisure (see 1 Sam 9.25-26).

11.4   Ritual of purification: from her menstrual period (see Lev 15.19-24).

11.8   A present: probably food from the royal table.

11.11   Covenant Box: see 1 Sam 3.3.
         How could I...sleep with my wife?: while war was being waged a soldier was required to abstain from sex (see 1 Sam 21.5).

11.13   blanket; or cot.

11.21   Abimelech: see Judges 9.50-54.

12.23   Where he is: in Sheol, the world of the dead (see 1 Sam 2.6).

12.25   Jedidiah: this name in Hebrew means "Beloved of the LORD."

12.30   idol of the Ammonite god Molech; or Ammonite king.

12.31   Probable text (see 1 Chr 20.3) work at; Hebrew pass through.

13.1   Amnon: being David's oldest son (see 3.2), he would have succeeded his father as king; Absalom was David's third oldest son (see 3.3).

13.13   He will give me to you: it was still permitted for a man to marry his half sister (see Gen 20.12); later this was prohibited (see Lev 20.17; Deut 27.22).

13.16   Probable text To send me...a greater crime; Hebrew unclear.

13.18   long robe with full sleeves; or decorated robe (see Gen 37.3).
         Probable text in those days; Hebrew garments.

13.27   Some ancient translations Absalom prepared a banquet fit for a king; Hebrew does not have these words.

13.34   Probable text from Horonaim; Hebrew behind him.
         One ancient translation He went...had seen; Hebrew does not have these words.

13.37-38   Talmai: Absalom's maternal grandfather (see 3.3).

13.39   Absalom: apparently now the heir to the throne; David's second son, Chileab (see 3.3), is not mentioned, and probably died in infancy.

14.2   Tekoa: about 16 kilometers south of Jerusalem.

(49)

14.14   Probable text Even God...from exile; Hebrew unclear.

14.17   can distinguish good from evil; or knows everything.

14.19   there is...question; or you are absolutely right.

15.7   Some ancient translations four; Hebrew forty.

15.8   One ancient translation in Hebron; Hebrew does not have these
words.

15.12   Gilo: a village near Hebron.

15.18   Probable text stood; Hebrew passed.
Gath: one of the five Philistine cities (see 1 Sam 6.17).

15.20   One ancient translation and may the LORD be kind and faithful
to you; Hebrew kindness and faithfulness.

15.23   Kidron Brook: east of Jerusalem.

15.24   Covenant Box: see 1 Sam 3.3.
Probable text set it down; Hebrew poured it out.
Probable text was there too; Hebrew went up.

15.27   Some ancient translations Look; Hebrew Are you the seer?

15.30   Mount of Olives: east of Jerusalem, on the other side of Kidron
Brook (verse 23).

15.31   One ancient translation was told; Hebrew told.

16.12   Some ancient translations misery; Hebrew wickedness.

16.14   One ancient translation the Jordan; Hebrew does not have these
words.

16.22   Absalom...had intercourse with his father's concubines: as predicted by the prophet Nathan (see 12.11-12); by doing this Absalom
was demonstrating that he was now the king (see 3.7).

17.3   One ancient translation like a bride...only one man; Hebrew like
the return of the whole, so is the man you seek.

17.13   Some ancient translations the city; Hebrew him.

17.16   Cross the Jordan: to the east side.

17.18   Bahurim: about two kilometers northeast of Jerusalem.

17.23   His hometown: see 15.12.

17.25   One ancient translation (and see 1 Chr 2.17) Ishmaelite; Hebrew
Israelite.

17.28-29   Some ancient translations peas; Hebrew peas and roasted grain.

18.18   King's Valley: Kidron Valley, east of Jerusalem.
He had no son: but see 14.27.

19.11   Some ancient translations The news...David; Hebrew The news...
David, to his palace, and places this sentence at the end of the
verse.

19.15   Gilgal: about 8 kilometers from the west bank of the Jordan;
King David and his troops were on the east side of the river
(see 17.27).

19.18   Probable text They crossed; Hebrew The crossing crossed.

19.19   The wrong I did: see 16.5-14.

19.25   One ancient translation from; Hebrew at.

19.37   son; or servant.

19.39   Crossed the Jordan: to the west side.

20.1   Gilgal: see 19.15.

20.8   Gibeon: see 2.12.

20.14   Abel Beth Maacah: in the extreme north of the country, not far
from the city of Dan.
Probable text Bikri; Hebrew Beri.

21.1   Consulted the LORD: see 1 Sam 14.36.
He put the people of Gibeon to death: there is no record of this
event.

21.9   Late in the spring: the end of April or beginning of May.

21.12   They had stolen them: see 1 Sam 31.8-13.

21.19   Probable text (see 1 Chr 20.5) Jair; Hebrew Jaaroregim.
Killed Goliath: in 1 Sam 17.41-54 Goliath's death is attributed
to David.
Loom: see 1 Sam 17.7.

22.6   The grave: Sheol, the world of the dead (see 1 Sam 2.6).

22.7   His temple: God's dwelling in heaven (see verses 10-11).

22.8   Foundations of the sky: the sky was thought of as an inverted
bowl supported by columns that extended down through the earth
into the underworld.

22.11   Winged creature: a creature associated with God's majesty and
presence (see Psa 18.10).

22.12   Some ancient translations (and see Psa 18.11) full of; Hebrew
unclear.

22.16   Foundations of the earth: it was believed that the surface of
the earth was supported by pillars which rested on a foundation
in the depths of the seas.

22.17   The deep waters: a figure of extreme danger (see verse 5).

22.26   Probable text (see Psa 18.25) those; Hebrew the strong.

22.29   Light: a figure of life and vitality.

22.33   Probable text (see Psa 18.32) he makes; Hebrew unclear.

22.46   Probable text (see Psa 18.45) come trembling; Hebrew come ready
to fight.

23.7   Verses 6-7 in Hebrew are unclear.

23.8   One ancient translation "The Three"; Hebrew the third.
Probable text (see 1 Chr 11.11) he fought with his spear;
Hebrew unclear.

23.13   Probable text Near the beginning of harvest time; Hebrew unclear.
Adullam Cave: see 1 Sam 22.1.
Rephaim Valley: see 5.18.

23.18   Zeruiah: see 1 Sam 26.6.
One ancient translation "The Thirty"; Hebrew The Three.

23.19   Probable text "The Thirty"; Hebrew The Three.

23.22   Probable text "The Thirty"; Hebrew The Three.

24.5   Probable text Aroer...Gad; Hebrew unclear.

24.6   One ancient translation Kadesh, in Hittite territory; Hebrew to
the land of Tahtim; Hodshi.
Probable text and from Dan they went; Hebrew unclear.

24.11-12   Gad, David's prophet: see 1 Sam 22.5.

24.13   Some ancient translations (and see 1 Chr 21.12) Three; Hebrew
Seven.

24.18   Araunah's threshing place: on the hill outside the old city of
Jerusalem; it was the place where Solomon later built the Temple
(see 1 Chr 22.1; 2 Chr 3.1).

24.23   Probable text to the king; Hebrew to the king the king.

24.25   Fellowship offerings: see 1 Sam 11.15.

1 KINGS

1.1   Very old man: probably about 70 years old.

1.3   Shunem: a town about 26 kilometers southwest of the southern end
of Lake Galilee.

1.5-6   Oldest surviving son: for Amnon's death, see 2 Sam 13.23-29, and
for Absalom's death, see 2 Sam 18.9-15; it appears that Chileab
(see 2 Sam 3.3-4) had died in infancy. Adonijah was David's fourth
son.

1.9   Spring of Enrogel: southeast of Jerusalem.
Sacrificial feast: celebrating Adonijah's claim to be king.

1.25   One ancient translation Joab the commander of your army; Hebrew
your army commanders.

1.33   Gihon Spring: a short distance (verse 41) north of Enrogel
Spring (verse 9); it was the principal source of water for
Jerusalem.

1.39   Tent of the LORD's presence: the place of worship, where God met
his people (see Exo 26); it was used until Solomon built the Temple
in Jerusalem.

1.50   Corners of the altar: projections at the four corners of the
altar that looked like horns. Anyone holding on to them was safe
from being killed.

2.5   Killing...Abner...and Amasa: see 2 Sam 3.22-27; 20.8-10.
Some ancient translations innocent men; Hebrew men in battle.
Some ancient translations I bear...and I suffer; Hebrew he bears
...and he suffers.

2.7   They were kind to me: see 2 Sam 17.27-29.

2.8   Shimei: see 2 Sam 16.5-13; 19.16-23.

2.10   David's City: the old part of Jerusalem, on Mount Zion, which
David had conquered from the Jebusites, the original inhabitants
(see 2 Sam 5.6-9).

2.15   I should have become king: Adonijah was older than Solomon (see Verse 22).

2.26   Anathoth: a Levitical city (see Josh 21.18) about 4 kilometers northeast of Jerusalem.
Covenant Box: a wooden chest covered with gold, in which were kept the two stone tablets on which were inscribed the Ten Commandments (see Exo 37.1-9).

2.27   What the LORD had said: see 1 Sam 2.27-36; Abiathar was great-grandson of Phinehas, the younger son of Eli (see 1 Sam 22.20; 22.9; 14.3; 1.3).

2.28   Corners of the altar: see 1.50.

2.29   One ancient translation Solomon sent a messenger...sent Benaiah; Hebrew Solomon sent Benaiah.

2.32   will punish...committed; or will kill Joab, because he committed those murders.
Abner...and Amasa: see 2.5.

2.37   Kidron Brook: immediately to the east of the city.

2.39   Gath: one of the five Philistine cities, near the Mediterranean coast.

3.1   David's City: see 2.10.

3.4   Gibeon: about 10 kilometers northwest of Jerusalem.

3.15   Covenant Box: see 2.26.

4.28   when it was needed; or wherever King Solomon was.

5.1   Tyre: a Phoenician city on the Mediterranean coast, north of Palestine.
A friend of David's: see 2 Sam 5.11-12.

5.11   Some ancient translations (and see 2 Chr 2.10) 110,000 gallons; Hebrew 1,100 gallons.

5.14   Adoniram: see 4.6b.

5.18   Byblos: an ancient Phoenician city on the Mediterranean coast, north of Tyre.

6.1   Fourth year of Solomon's reign: about 960 B.C.
Ziv: the Jewish month that began with the first new moon occurring after the modern April 10.

6.8   Some ancient translations lowest; Hebrew middle.

6.10   Probable text three-storied annex, each story; Hebrew three-storied annex.

6.16   One ancient translation ceiling; Hebrew walls.

6.19   Covenant Box: see 2.26.

6.20   Altar: the one on which incense was burned.
Verse 20 in Hebrew is unclear.

6.23   Winged creatures: figures which symbolized God's majesty and were associated with his presence with his people; see a description of them in Exo 25.18-20.

6.38   Bul: the Jewish month that began with the first new moon occurring after the modern October 4.

7.2-3   Hall of the Forest of Lebanon: a large ceremonial hall in the palace, probably so called because it was paneled in cedar.
One ancient translation three; Hebrew four.

7.5   One ancient translation windows; Hebrew doorposts.

7.7   Some ancient translations rafters; Hebrew floor.

7.15   Some ancient translations each one...circumference; Hebrew the first column was 27 feet tall and the second column was 18 feet in circumference.

7.17   Verse 17 in Hebrew is unclear.

7.20   One ancient translation each; Hebrew the second.

7.21   Jachin: this name sounds like the Hebrew for "he (God) establishes."
Boaz: this name sounds like the Hebrew for "by his (God's) strength."

7.24   Probable text All around...tank; Hebrew unclear.

7.48   The bread offered to God: see Lev 24.5-8.

8.1   Covenant Box: see 2.26.
David's City: see 2.10.

8.2   Festival of Shelters: celebrated in the fall after the completion of the harvest. In remembrance of the years when their ancestors wandered through the wilderness, the Israelites constructed rough shelters in which to live during the eight-day celebration. The Jewish name for this festival is Sukkoth (the Hebrew name for "shelters").
Ethanim: corresponding to modern mid-September to mid-October.

8.4   Tent of the LORD's presence: see 1.39.

8.6   Winged creatures: see 6.23.

8.12   One ancient translation You...sky; Hebrew does not have these
words.
        Darkness: the Most Holy Place had no windows and no natural
light penetrated it except when the door was open.

8.63   Fellowship offerings: sacrifices in which only part of the
animal was burned on the altar; the rest was eaten by the
worshipers.

8.65   One ancient translation seven; Hebrew fourteen.

9.2   As he had: see 3.5-6.

9.5   When I told him: see 2 Sam 7.12-16.

9.8   Some ancient translations a pile of ruins; Hebrew high.

9.13   Cabul: this name sounds like "ke-bal," the Hebrew for "worthless."

9.21   The present time: the time of the writing of this book.

9.24   David's City: see 2.10.

9.25   Hebrew has two additional words, the meaning of which is unclear.

9.28   Ophir: perhaps in what is now southern Arabia.

10.1   Sheba: probably in what is now southwest Arabia.
        Probable text (see 2 Chr 9.1) Solomon's fame; Hebrew Solomon's
fame concerning the name of the LORD.

10.6   you; or your deeds.

10.8   Some ancient translations wives; Hebrew men.

10.15   Some ancient translations taxes; Hebrew men.

10.17   Hall of the Forest of Lebanon: see 7.2-3.

10.22   monkeys; or peacocks.

10.28   Probable text Musri; Hebrew Egypt.
        Musri and Cilicia: two ancient countries in what is now south-
east Turkey which were centers of horse breeding in Solomon's time.

11.3   Concubines: female servants who, although not wives, had sexual
relations with their masters. They had important legal rights, and
their masters were referred to as their husbands.

11.22   One ancient translation And he went back to his country; Hebrew
does not have these words.
   One ancient translation As king...Israel; in Hebrew this sentence,
with some differences, comes at the end of verse 25.

11.24   Hadadezer and...his Syrian allies: see 2 Sam 8.3-6; 10.15-19.

11.26   Zeredah: some 45 kilometers northwest of Jerusalem.

11.32   One tribe: by this time the tribe of Judah had taken over the
territory of the tribe of Simeon, so that the two tribes were
considered one (see Josh 19.1,9).

11.33   Some ancient translations Solomon has...and has; Hebrew they
have...and have.
   Some ancient translations Solomon has; Hebrew They have.

11.43   David's City: see 2.10.

12.1   Shechem: the chief city of the northern tribes, some 50 kilometers
north of Jerusalem (see Josh 24.1).

12.2   Some ancient translations (and see 2 Chr 10.2) returned from;
Hebrew remained in.

12.15   What he had spoken: see 11.29-39.

12.25   Penuel: in Gilead, on the east side of the Jordan River.

12.29   Bethel...Dan: towns in the extreme south and the extreme north
of the northern kingdom of Israel.

12.30   One ancient translation in Bethel and in Dan; Hebrew in Dan.

12.32   Eighth month: Bul, the Jewish month that began with the first new
moon occurring after the modern October 4.
   Festival in Judah: the Festival of Shelters, celebrated in Judah
on the 15th day of the seventh month (see 8.2).

13.2   Josiah: King Josiah of Judah, who ruled 640-609 B.C. (see
2 Kgs 22.1--23.30).

13.11   Some ancient translations sons; Hebrew son.

13.12   Some ancient translations showed him; Hebrew saw.

13.32   Samaria: it was only some 50 years after this that the city of
Samaria was founded (see 16.23-24), and only much later was the
name given to the northern kingdom of Israel (see 2 Kgs 17.24).

14.2   Ahijah...who said: see 11.29-39.

14.10   young and old; or slave and free.

14.14   Hebrew has five additional words, the meaning of which is unclear.

14.15   Asherah: a Canaanite goddess of fertility; her male counterpart was Baal.

14.17   Tirzah: some 10 kilometers northeast of Shechem (see 12.1); it was the capital of the northern kingdom of Israel until Samaria was built (see 16.24).

14.25   Fifth year of Rehoboam's reign: about 926 B.C.

14.31   David's City: see 2.10.

15.5   Uriah the Hittite: see 2 Sam 11.2-27.

15.6   Abijah; most Hebrew manuscripts have Rehoboam (as in 14.30).

15.8   David's City: see 2.10.

15.17   Ramah: in the hill country of Ephraim, some 8 kilometers north of Jerusalem.

15.29   The LORD had said: see 14.7-11.

15.33   Ahijah: see verse 27; not the prophet from Shiloh (verse 29).

16.12   The LORD had said: see verses 1-4.

16.31   Sidon: a Phoenician city on the Mediterranean coast, north of Palestine.
        Baal: a Canaanite fertility god; his female counterpart was Asherah.

16.33   Asherah: see 14.15.

16.34   The LORD had foretold: see Josh 6.26.
        Laid the foundation...built the gates: it is possible that Hiel's two sons were killed and their bodies buried in the foundation and under the gate as a means of securing the gods' favor.

17.1   Gilead: on the east side of the Jordan River.
        No dew or rain: to prove that it was Yahweh, the God of Israel, and not Baal, the god of Sidon (see 16.31-32), who controlled the weather.

17.9   Zarephath: some 15 kilometers south of Sidon (see 16.31).

18.5   One ancient translation Let us go and look; Hebrew You go and look.

18.15   Almighty: a title which refers to God as the commander of Israel's armies (see 1 Sam 17.45) or of the heavenly powers.

18.18   Baal: see 16.31.

18.19   Asherah: see 14.15.

18.20   Mount Carmel: near the Mediterranean coast, immediately south of the Phoenician plain, north of Palestine.

18.31   The LORD had given the name Israel: see Gen 32.28; 35.10.

18.36   The hour of the afternoon sacrifice: around 3:00 P.M.

18.37   you are bringing them back to yourself; or you yourself made them turn away from you.

18.45   Jezreel: some 27 kilometers southeast of Mount Carmel.

19.3   Beersheba: the southernmost city in Judah, some 210 kilometers south of Jezreel.

19.14   Almighty: see 18.15.

19.16   Jehu son of Nimshi: in 2 Kgs 9.2 he is said to be Nimshi's grandson.

19.20   all right...you; or Go on, but come back, because what I have just done to you is important.

20.1   King Benhadad: successor of the King Benhadad in 15.8-20.

20.6   Some ancient translations they; Hebrew you.

20.21   One ancient translation captured; Hebrew destroyed.

20.26   Aphek: perhaps east of Lake Galilee, in the north.

21.3   Inherited: according to the Law of Moses, land was to remain in the possession of the descendants of the original owner.

21.13   Two: the law required at least two accusing witnesses (see Deut 17.6-7).
    Cursing God: a crime punishable by death (see Exo 22.28; Lev 24.10-16).

22.3   Gilead: on the east side of the Jordan River.

22.38   The LORD had said: see 21.19.

22.48   Eziongeber: a port at the northern end of the Gulf of Aqaba (see 9.26).

1 Kgs 24.50--2 Kgs 4.8

24.50   David's City: see 2.10.

24.53   Baal: see 16.31.

2 KINGS

1.1   Moab: on the east side of the Dead Sea.

1.2   Roof: at that time roofs were flat and were used as a place for
rest and leisure.
        Baalzebub: this name in Hebrew means "lord of the flies," an
insulting pun on the name Baalzebul, which means "Baal the Prince."
The title "Baal" itself means "lord" or "god."

1.8   was wearing...with; or was a hairy man and wore.

1.11   One ancient translation went up; Hebrew answered.

1.17   Some ancient translations his brother; Hebrew does not have
these words.

2.1   Gilgal: some 13 kilometers north of Bethel (verse 2).

2.8   The other side: the east side.

2.9   The share...successor: Elisha asked for the share that the oldest
son inherited by law from his father (see Deut 21.17).

3.4   Moab: see 1.1.

3.8   Edom: to the south of the Dead Sea; the plan was to go around
the Dead Sea and attack Moab from the south.

3.13   Those prophets: that is, the prophets of Baal.
        Your father and mother: Ahab and Jezebel (verses 1,2).

3.20   Time of the regular morning sacrifice: around 9:00 A.M.

3.24   One ancient translation kept up the pursuit; Hebrew unclear.

3.25   Probable text only the capital city of Kir Heres; Hebrew unclear.
        Slingers: men who used hand slings to throw stones.

3.26   One ancient translation Syria; Hebrew Edom.
        Terrified: either because of what Chemosh, the god of the
Moabites, might do, or because of what the LORD, the God of the
Israelites, might do.

4.8   Shunem: about 26 kilometers southwest of the southern end of
Lake Galilee.

4.23   Sabbath...New Moon Festival: more appropriate times for consulting a prophet.

4.25   Mount Carmel: about 32 kilometers northwest of Shunem.

4.38   Gilgal: see 2.1.

5.3   The prophet who lives in Samaria: Elisha.

5.5   The king of Israel: Joram (see 3.1).

5.7   God; or a god.

5.11   the diseased spot; or this place.

5.17   Earth to take home with me: it was believed that a god could be
worshiped only on his own land.

6.13   Dothan: about 15 kilometers north of Samaria.

6.25   Dove's dung: this may have been the popular name for some common
food such as wild onions or chickpeas.

6.33   Probable text king; Hebrew messenger.

7.6   Egyptian; or Musrite (see 1 Kgs 10.28).

7.13   Verse 13 in Hebrew is unclear.

8.13   You will be king of Syria: as God had announced to Elijah
(see 1 Kgs 19.15).

8.16   Some ancient translations Israel; Hebrew Israel, Jehoshaphat
being king of Judah.

8.22   independent of; or in revolt against.
        Libnah: about 20 kilometers west of Jerusalem, near the Philistine
border.

8.24   David's City: see 1 Kgs 2.10.

8.28   Gilead: on the east side of the Jordan.

8.29   Jezreel: in northern Israel, about 65 kilometers from Ramoth.

9.6   I anoint you king...of Israel: as God had announced to Elijah
(see 1 Kgs 19.16).

9.7   The king, that son of Ahab: King Joram of Israel (see 3.1).

9.14-15   Was in Jezreel: see 8.28-29.

9.21   The field which had belonged to Naboth: see 1 Kgs 21.

9.27   Some ancient translations and they wounded him; Hebrew does not have these words.
        Megiddo: about 15 kilometers northwest of Jezreel.

9.28   David's City: see 1 Kgs 2.10.

9.31   Zimri: the Israelite army officer who assassinated King Elah of Israel (see 1 Kgs 16.8-12).

9.36   The LORD said: see 1 Kgs 21.23.

10.1   Some ancient translations the city; Hebrew Jezreel.

10.10 The LORD said: see 1 Kgs 21.21-22.

10.18 Baal: a Canaanite fertility god.

10.21 Temple of Baal: built by King Ahab, husband of Jezebel (see 1 Kgs 16.32).

10.27 Today: the time of the writing of the account.

10.29 The gold bull-calves: see 1 Kgs 12.28-30.

11.1   King Ahaziah's mother Athaliah: daughter of King Ahab of Israel and widow of King Jehoram of Judah (see 8.18,26).

11.2   Jehosheba: according to 2 Chr 22.11 she was the wife of the priest Jehoiada (see verse 4, below).

11.6   Hebrew has an additional word, the meaning of which is unclear.

11.10 Some ancient translations (and see 2 Chr 23.9) spears; Hebrew spear.

11.12 a copy of laws governing kingship; or royal insignia or bracelets.

12.10 melt down the silver, and weigh it; or count the money, and tie it up in bags.

12.16 Repayment offerings: for the nature and purpose of these offerings, see Lev 5.14--6.7.

12.17 Gath: one of the five Philistine cities, near the Mediterranean coast.

12.20-21 David's City: see 1 Kgs 2.10.

13.5   A leader: identity unknown.

13.6   Some ancient translations kept on; Hebrew he kept on.
Asherah: a Canaanite goddess of fertility; her male counterpart was Baal.

13.14   The mighty defender of Israel: the same words applied by Elisha
to Elijah (see 2.12).

13.21   One ancient translation and ran off; Hebrew and he ran off.

14.6   The Law of Moses: see Deut 24.16.

14.8   challenging him to fight; or inviting him to a conference.

14.11   Beth Shemesh: some 24 kilometers southwest of Jerusalem.

14.15-16   These two verses are the same as 13.12-13, and do not belong
here.

14.19   Lachish: some 35 kilometers southwest of Jerusalem.

14.20   David's City: see 1 Kgs 2.10.

14.22   Elath: the port at the northern end of the Gulf of Aqaba.

14.26   Some ancient translations terrible; Hebrew rebellious.

14.28   One ancient translation to Israel; Hebrew for Judah in Israel.

15.7   David's City: see 1 Kgs 2.10.

15.10   One ancient translation at Ibleam; Hebrew before people.

15.12   Fourth generation: Zechariah was Jehu's great-great-grandson.

15.14   Tirzah: former capital of the northern kingdom of Israel
(see 1 Kgs 16.23-24).

15.16   One ancient translation Tappuah; Hebrew Tiphsah.

15.25   Hebrew has two additional words, the meaning of which is unclear.

15.38   David's City: see 1 Kgs 2.10.

16.6   Probable text the king of Edom; Hebrew King Rezin of Syria.
Elath: see 14.22.
Still live there: at the time of the writing of the account.

16.17   The bronze carts: see 1 Kgs 7.27-39.
The bronze tank: see 1 Kgs 7.23-26.

16.18   Verse 18 in Hebrew is unclear.

16.20   David's City: see 1 Kgs 2.10.

17.4   So, king of Egypt; or the king of Egypt at Sais.

17.6   Assyrian emperor: probably Sargon II, the successor of
Shalmaneser.
Captured Samaria: in 722 B.C.

17.8   Probable text and adopted...Israel; Hebrew unclear.

17.9   did; or said.

17.16   Asherah: see 13.6.
Baal: see 10.18.

17.23   They still live: at the time of the writing of the account.

17.24   Samaria: the name of the capital city is now applied to the
whole territory of the former kingdom of Israel.

17.27   Some ancient translations him; Hebrew them.

17.34   This day: the time of the writing of the account.

18.4   Asherah: see 13.6.
Moses had made: see Num 21.9.

18.11   Assyrian emperor: see 17.6.

18.13   Fourteenth year: 701 B.C.

18.14   Lachish: see 14.19.

18.26   Aramaic: the language of Syria (Aram), which had become the
common language of the various peoples of that part of the world.

18.34   Hamath and Arpad: cities in Syria.
Sepharvaim, Hena, and Ivvah: cities whose location is uncertain.
Samaria: see 17.24.

19.8   Lachish: see 18.14.

19.15   Winged creatures: see 1 Kgs 6.23.

19.26   Probable text when the hot east wind blasts them; Hebrew blasted
before they are grown.

19.37   Ararat: in what later became Armenia (now a part of Turkey).

20.7   One ancient translation (and see Isa 38.21) figs, and he would
get well; Hebrew figs. They did so and he got well.

20.9   Stairway...steps...steps; or sundial...degrees...degrees.

20.10   steps...steps; or degrees...degrees.

20.11   steps...stairway; or degrees...sundial. Archaeologial evidence
suggests that the stairway referred to in this passage was one
specially constructed to tell time.

20.18   Made eunuchs: castrated.

20.20   A tunnel: dug through 520 meters (1700 feet) of solid rock, it
brought the water down from Gihon Spring (see 1 Kgs 1.33), outside
the city walls, to Siloam Pool, inside the city walls.

21.3   Baal...Asherah: see 10.18; 13.6.

21.6   consulted; or brought back.

21.7   The LORD had said: see 1 Kgs 9.3-5.

21.13   As I did Samaria: see 17.5-23.

22.8   The book of the Law: probably a part, if not all, of what is
now Deuteronomy.

22.14   Newer part: to the northwest of the Temple.

22.20   Die in peace: actually Josiah died in battle (see 23.29-30).

23.2   Book of the covenant: see 22.8.

23.4   Baal...Asherah: see 10.18; 13.6.
Kidron Valley: to the east of the city.

23.5   Some ancient translations offer sacrifices; Hebrew and he offered
sacrifices.

23.7   Temple prostitutes: men and women who practiced prostitution in
the worship of fertility gods.

23.10   Hinnom Valley: to the south of the city.
Molech: see verse 13.

23.12   Probable text smashed...to bits; Hebrew unclear.

23.13   Mount of Olives: Hebrew here refers to it as "Mount of Destruction" or "Mount of Sin."

23.15   Had been built by King Jeroboam: see 1 Kgs 12.32-33.
One ancient translation broke its stones into pieces; Hebrew
burned the altar.

23.16   The prophet had predicted: see 1 Kgs 13.2-3.
One ancient translation during the festival...the prophet;
Hebrew does not have these words.

(65)

23.18   The prophet who had come from Samaria: he was from Bethel itself
(so 1 Kgs 13.11,31), which was in the northern kingdom of Israel,
at this time called Samaria.

23.29   Megiddo: about 40 kilometers southwest of the southern end of
Lake Galilee (see 9.27-28).

23.31   Jeremiah: not the prophet of the same name.

23.33   Riblah: on the Orontes River, in what is now Syria.

23.34   Changed his name: to show that the king of Judah was subject to
the king of Egypt.

24.17   Changed his name: see 23.34.

24.18   Jeremiah: see 23.31.

25.1   Tenth month of the ninth year: January 588 B.C.

25.2   Eleventh year: 587 B.C.

25.3   Probable text (see Jer 52.6) the fourth month; Hebrew the month.
The fourth month: equivalent to modern mid-June to mid-July.

25.6   Riblah: see 23.33.

25.11   Probable text (see Jer 52.15) skilled workmen; Hebrew crowd.

25.13   Bronze columns...the carts...large bronze tank: see 1 Kgs 7.15-39.

25.23   Mizpah: about 12 kilometers north of Jerusalem.

25.27   Twelfth month: Adar, the Jewish month that began with a new moon
occurring in modern February.

1 CHRONICLES

1.5   The names Gomer, Magog, Madai, etc. in verses 5-23 stand both
for individuals and for nations. In some instances it is possible
to identify the nations by their proper names (see verses 7-8);
Javan (verse 5) may be Greece (see Gen 10.4-5).

1.19   Eber: the name from which "Hebrew" is derived.
Peleg: this name sounds like the Hebrew for "divide."

1.32   Concubine: a female servant who, although not a wife, had sexual
relations with her master. She had important legal rights, and her
master was referred to as her husband.

1.38-42   Edom: the country south of the Dead Sea, also known as Seir,
inhabited by the descendants of Esau.

1.43-50   Rehoboth-on-the-River: the "River" is the Euphrates.

2.3   Bathshua; or daughter of Shua.
Er: see Gen 38.2-7.

2.4   Tamar: see Gen 38.12-30.

2.7   Achan: this is his name in Josh 7.1. The Hebrew text here calls him "Achar," which means "disaster."

2.13   Seven sons: according to 1 Sam 16.10-11; 17.12, Jesse had eight sons.

2.18   Some ancient translations had a daughter... She had; Hebrew unclear.

2.20   Bezalel: see Exo 31.1-5.

2.22   ruled; or owned.
Gilead: on the east side of the Jordan River.

2.24   Some ancient translations his son...widow; Hebrew unclear.

2.42   Probable text father of Mareshah...Hebron; Hebrew unclear.

2.46   Concubine: see 1.32.

3.1-3   See 2 Sam 3.2-5; instead of Daniel here, in 2 Sam 3.3 he is called Chileab.

3.9   Concubines: see 1.32.

3.17   Taken prisoner: see 2 Kgs 24.10-15.

3.21   Verse 21 in Hebrew is unclear.

4.3-4   Some ancient translations sons; Hebrew fathers.

4.9   Jabez: this name sounds like the Hebrew for "pain."

4.13   Some ancient translations Meneothai; Hebrew does not have this name.

4.19   Verse 19 in Hebrew is unclear.

4.22   Probable text settled in Bethlehem; Hebrew unclear.

4.39   Some ancient translations Gerar; Hebrew Gedor.
Gerar: on the southwest border of Canaan (see Gen 20.1; 26.17).

4.41   Hezekiah: see 2 Kgs 18-20; he ruled 716-687 B.C.

4.43   Ever since: to the time of the writing of the account.

5.1   Reuben: see Gen 35.22. Concubines: see 1.32.

5.2   A ruler: King David.

5.9   Gilead: see 2.22.

5.16   Sharon: not the better-known place south of Mount Carmel, but some place east of the Jordan River.

5.17   King Jotham: ruled 740-736 B.C.; King Jeroboam II: ruled 783-743 B.C.

5.18   Tribes of Reuben, Gad, and East Manasseh: the two and a half tribes that settled east of the Jordan River (see Num 32.28-33; Deut 3.12-13).

5.22   The exile: about 733 B.C. the Assyrians conquered northern Israel and the Israelite territory east of the Jordan River and deported the people (see 2 Kgs 15.29).

6.15   King Nebuchadnezzar: see 2 Kgs 25.1-7.

6.28   Some ancient translations (and see 1 Sam 8.2) Joel; Hebrew does not have this name.

6.32   Covenant Box: a wooden chest covered with gold, in which were kept the two stone tablets on which were inscribed the Ten Commandments (see Exo 37.1-9).
       Tent of the LORD's presence: the place of worship, where God met his people (see Exo 26); it was used until Solomon built the Temple in Jerusalem.
       King Solomon built the Temple: see 1 Kgs 6.

6.49   Most Holy Place: see 1 Kgs 6.19-28.

6.57-59   City of refuge: if anyone accidentally killed someone, he could escape to one of these cities and be safe from revenge (see Josh 20.1-9).

7.6   Benjamin: this list of descendants (verses 6-12a) may be that of Zebulun, which otherwise is missing; Benjamin's descendants are given in 8.1-12.

7.12   Probable text Shuppim...Hushim (see Gen 46.23; Num 26.39,42); Hebrew and Shuppim and Huppim, sons of Ir; Hushim son of Aher.

7.13   Bilhah: a concubine of Jacob and the mother of his two sons Dan and Naphtali (see Gen 30.1-8).

7.14   Concubine: see 1.32.

7.21   Gath: one of the five Philistine cities along the Mediterranean coast.

7.23   Beriah: this name sounds like the Hebrew for "in trouble."

7.35   Probable text (see verse 32) Hotham; Hebrew Helem.

8.3   Gera, Abihud; or Gera father of Ehud (see Judges 3.15).

8.29   Probable text (see 9.35) Jeiel; Hebrew does not have this name.

8.31   One ancient translation (and see 9.36) Ner; Hebrew does not have this name.

8.33   Eshbaal: called Ishbosheth in 2 Sam 2.8 and elsewhere in 2 Sam.

8.34   Meribaal: called Mephibosheth in 2 Sam 4.4 and elsewhere in 2 Sam.

9.1   The Book of the Kings of Israel: not the biblical book of Kings.

9.18   King's Gate: the east gate of the Temple, through which the king usually entered.

9.19   Tent of the LORD's presence: see 6.32.

9.20   Phinehas: see Num 25.6-13.

9.31   Baked offerings: thin cakes of flour and olive oil which were baked and then presented as offerings to God(see Lev 2.4-6).

9.32   Sacred bread: twelve loaves of bread which were placed on a table in the Temple each Sabbath as an offering to God (see Lev 24.5-9).

9.39   Eshbaal: see 8.33.

9.40   Meribaal: see 8.34.

9.41   Some ancient translations (and see 1 Chr 8.35) Ahaz; Hebrew does not have this name.

10.1   Mount Gilboa: some 32 kilometers southwest of Lake Galilee.

10.7   Jezreel Valley: to the north and east of Mount Gilboa.

10.11   Jabesh in Gilead: see 1 Sam 11.

10.13   Consulting the spirits of the dead: see 1 Sam 28.3-25.

11.1   Hebron: some 32 kilometers southwest of Jerusalem.

11.2   Zeruiah: see 2.16.

11.11   One ancient translation (and see 2 Sam 23.8) "The Three";
Hebrew "The Thirty."

11.15   Adullam Cave: see 1 Sam 22.1.
Rephaim Valley: see 2 Sam 5.18.

11.16   Bethlehem: David's home, some 8 kilometers south of Jerusalem.

11.20   One ancient translation Thirty; Hebrew Three.
One ancient translation (and see 2 Sam 23.18) "The Thirty";
Hebrew "The Three."

11.21   Probable text (see 2 Sam 23.19) most famous of "The Thirty";
Hebrew unclear.

11.24   Probable text "The Thirty"; Hebrew "The Three."

11.26-47   Probable text Hashem; Hebrew the sons of Hashem.
Probable text from Zobah; Hebrew unclear.

12.1   Ziklag: the town which the Philistine king of Gath had assigned
to David (see 1 Sam 27.5-6).

12.8   The desert fort: probably in Moab, on the east side of the
Jordan River (see 1 Sam 22.4); Gad was north of Moab.

12.19   Ziklag: see verse 1.

12.21   They served David...troops; or They helped David fight against
the band of raiders.

12.23-27   Hebron: see 11.1.

13.3   Covenant Box: see 6.31.

13.5   Kiriath Jearim: about 15 kilometers northwest of Jerusalem
(see 1 Sam 6.20--7.1).

13.6   The winged creatures: figures which symbolized God's majesty and
were associated with his presence with his people; see a description of them in Exo 25.18-20.

13.7   Ahio; or his brother.

13.11   Perez Uzzah: this name in Hebrew means "Punishment of Uzzah."

14.1   Tyre: a Phoenician city on the Mediterranean coast, north of
Palestine.

14.7   Beeliada: called Eliada in 3.8.

14.9   Rephaim Valley: probably southwest of Jerusalem.

14.10   Asked God: by means of the sacred stones carried in the ephod (see 1 Sam 2.28).

14.11   Baal Perazim: this name in Hebrew means "Lord of the Breakthrough."

15.1   David's City: that part of Jerusalem which David had captured from the original inhabitants, the Jebusites (see 2 Sam 5.6-10).

15.2   him; or it.

15.12   Purify yourselves: a ritual to remove any ceremonial impurity which prevented the proper performance of religious duties.

15.15   The LORD had commanded: see Exo 25.12-15.

15.27   Ephod: a garment ordinarily worn by a priest (see 1 Sam 2.28).

16.3   a piece of roasted meat; or a cake of dates.

16.5   Jeiel (the first one); probably Jaaziel (as in 15.17-21).

16.29   when he appears; or in garments of worship; or in his beautiful Temple.

16.39   Gibeon: about 10 kilometers northwest of Jerusalem (see 21.29).

17.1   Covenant Box: see 6.31.

17.16   Tent of the LORD's presence: see 6.32.

17.17   Probable text and you, LORD God...man; Hebrew unclear.

17.24   Almighty: a title which refers to God as the commander of Israel's armies or of the heavenly powers.

18.3   Zobah: a region north of Damascus.

18.6   set up military camps in; or placed military commanders over.

18.8   The tank, the columns, and the bronze utensils: see 1 Kgs 7.15-26, 40-45.

18.9   Hamath: a region north of Zobah (verse 3).

18.13   set up military camps; or placed military commanders.
Edom: the country south of the Dead Sea; the Edomites were descendants of Esau.

18.16   Probable text (see 2 Sam 8.17) Seraiah; Hebrew Shavsha.

19.1   Ammon: a land on the east side of the Dead Sea.

(71)

19.7 Medeba: a town about 20 kilometers east of the north end of the Dead Sea.

20.2 Ammonite idol Molech; or Ammonite king.

20.5 Lahmi, the brother of Goliath: 2 Sam 21.19 has Goliath as the slain giant.

20.6 Loom: a device used for weaving cloth from thread or yarn.

21.1 Satan: the ruler of the forces of evil; the name means "the opponent" (see Job 1.6-12; Zech 3.1-2).

21.18 Araunah's threshing place: on the hill outside the old city of Jerusalem; it was the place where Solomon later built the Temple (see 22.1; 2 Chr 3.1).

21.26 Fellowship offerings: sacrifices in which only a part of the animal was burned on the altar; the rest was eaten by the worshipers. Fire from heaven: a sign of God's approval of David's choice of the place as the site of the future Temple.

21.29 Tent of the LORD's presence: see 6.32.
Gibeon: see 16.39.

22.4 Tyre and Sidon: Phoenician cities on the Mediterranean coast, north of Palestine.

22.9 Solomon: this name is formed from the Hebrew word "shalom," which means "peace and security."

22.14 by my efforts; or despite my poverty.

22.19 Covenant Box: see 6.31.

23.9 Shimei...Haran: the relation of this list to the list of Shimei's sons in verse 10 is not clear.

23.26 Tent of the LORD's presence: see 6.32.

24.7-18 8) Abijah: the order to which Zechariah, father of John the Baptist, belonged (see Luke 1.5).

26.20 One ancient translation fellow Levites; Hebrew Levites, Ahijah.

26.31 Gilead: on the east side of the Jordan River.

27.2-15 Probable text Mikloth...command; Hebrew unclear.
Succeeded him: Asahel was killed before David became king of the whole country (see 2 Sam 2.18-23), and his son took his place.

27.34 Ahithophel died: he committed suicide (see 2 Sam 17.23).

28.2　　Covenant Box: see 6.31.

28.11　Most Holy Place: see 1 Kgs 6.16,19-28.

28.18　Winged creatures: see 13.6.

29.22　Second time: see 23.1 for the first time.

2 CHRONICLES

1.3　　Gibeon: see 1 Chr 16.39.
　　　Tent of the LORD's presence: see 1 Chr 6.32.

1.4　　Covenant Box: see 1 Chr 6.31.
　　　Brought...from Kiriath Jearim: see 1 Chr 13.5-14; 15.25--16.1.

1.13　Some ancient translations left; Hebrew came to.

1.16　Probable text Musri; Hebrew Egypt.
　　　Musri and Cilicia: two ancient countries in what is now southeast Turkey which were centers of horse breeding in Solomon's time.

1.17　Verses 16-17 in Hebrew are unclear.

2.3　　Tyre: a Phoenician city on the Mediterranean coast, north of Palestine.

2.16　Joppa: on the Mediterranean coast, about 60 kilometers from Jerusalem.

3.1　　Araunah the Jebusite: see 1 Chr 21.18--22.1.

3.2　　Second month: named Ziv, the Jewish month that began with the first new moon occurring after the modern April 10.
　　　Fourth year that he was king: about 960 B.C.

3.6　　Parvaim: location unknown; perhaps Arabia.

3.7　　Winged creatures: see 1 Chr 13.6.

3.16　Verse 16 in Hebrew is unclear.

3.17　Jachin: this name sounds like the Hebrew for "he (God) establishes."
　　　Boaz: this name sounds like the Hebrew for "by his (God's) strength."

4.3　　Probable text All around...tank; Hebrew unclear.
　　　Bulls: in 1 Kgs 7.24 gourds.

4.11-16   Probable text (see 1 Kgs 7.40-45) ten; Hebrew he made.
          One ancient translation all these objects; Hebrew all their
     objects.

4.17   Zeredah: in 1 Kgs 7.46 Zarethan.

4.19   The bread offered to God: see Lev 24.5-8.

5.2   Covenant Box: see 1 Chr 6.31.
          David's City: that part of Jerusalem which David had captured
     from the original inhabitants, the Jebusites (see 2 Sam 5.6-10).

5.3   Festival of Shelters: celebrated in the fall after the comple-
     tion of the harvest. In remembrance of the years when their
     ancestors wandered through the wilderness, the Israelites construct-
     ed rough shelters in which to live during the eight-day celebration.
     The Jewish name for this festival is Sukkoth (the Hebrew name for
     "shelters").

5.5   Tent of the LORD's presence: see 1 Chr 6.32.

5.7   Winged creatures: see 3.10-13.

5.9   Today: at the time of the writing of the account.

6.1   Darkness: the Most Holy Place had no windows and no natural
     light penetrated it except when the curtain was drawn.

6.42   the love you...David; or your servant David's loyal service.

7.1   Fire...from heaven: see 1 Chr 21.26.

7.5   Fellowship offerings: sacrifices in which only a part of the
     animal was burned on the altar; the rest was eaten by the worshipers.

7.8   Festival of Shelters: see 5.3.

7.10   Seventh month: Ethanim, the Jewish month that began with the
     first new moon occurring after the modern September 4.

8.3   Hamath and Zobah: north of Damascus.

8.4   Palmyra: in an oasis some 190 kilometers northeast of Damascus;
     1 Kgs 9.18 speaks of Tamar, in Judah.

8.8   The present time: the time of the writing of the account.

8.11   David's City: see 5.2.
          Covenant Box: see 1 Chr 6.31.

8.13   Festival of Unleavened Bread: see 30.13.
        Harvest Festival: celebrated fifty days after Passover, at the
end of the wheat harvest. The Jewish name for this festival is
Shavuoth (the Feast of Weeks); its Christian name is Pentecost.
        Festival of Shelters: see 5.3.

8.18   Ophir: perhaps in what is now southern Arabia.

9.1   Sheba: probably in what is now southwest Arabia.

9.4   Probable text (see 1 Kgs 10.5) sacrifices he offered; Hebrew
his upper rooms.

9.5   you; or your deeds.

9.12   Probable text he gave her in exchange for the gifts; Hebrew
unclear.

9.16   Hall of the Forest of Lebanon: a large ceremonial hall in the
palace probably so called because it was paneled in cedar.

9.21   monkeys; or peacocks.

9.28   Probable text (see 1.16) Musri; Hebrew Egypt.

9.31   David's City: see 5.2.

10.1   Shechem: the chief city of the northern tribes, some 50 kilometers
north of Jerusalem (see Josh 24.1).

10.15   What he had spoken: see 1 Kgs 11.29-39.

11.21   Concubines: female servants who, although not wives, had sexual
relations with their masters. They had important legal rights, and
their masters were referred to as their husbands.

12.16   David's City: see 5.2.

13.8   The gold bull-calves that Jeroboam made: see 1 Kgs 12.28-30.

14.1   David's City: see 5.2.

14.3   Asherah: a Canaanite goddess of fertility; her male counterpart
was Baal.

14.13   Gerar: in the southwest of Judah, near the border with Philistia.
        So many of the Sudanese...fight; or The Sudanese were completely
defeated; not one of them was left alive.

15.3   a law; or the Law.

15.8   Some ancient translations Azariah son of; Hebrew does not have
these words.

(75)

15.10   Third month: Sivan, the Jewish month that began with the first new moon occurring after the modern May 9.

15.16   Asherah: see 14.3.
Kidron Valley: to the east of Jerusalem.

16.1   Ramah: in the hill country of Ephraim, some 8 kilometers north of Jerusalem.

16.7   One ancient translation Israel; Hebrew Syria.

16.14   David's City: see 5.2.

17.3   Baal: a Canaanite god of fertility; his female counterpart was Asherah.

17.6   Asherah: see 14.3.

17.9   The book of the Law of the LORD: probably a part, if not all, of the Pentateuch, the first five books of the Old Testament.

18.1   A member of his family: his son Jehoram married Athaliah, daughter of Ahab (see 21.6; 22.2-3).

18.2   Gilead: on the east side of the Jordan River.

19.3   Asherah: see 14.3.

19.8   Some ancient translations between...city; Hebrew unclear.

20.1   Moab and Ammon: countries on the east side of the Jordan.
One ancient translation Meunites; Hebrew Ammonites.
Meunites: probably an Arab tribe.

20.2   Edom: a country south of the Dead Sea.
Engedi: on the west shore of the Dead Sea.

20.9   struck them to punish them--a war; or struck them--a devastating war.

20.16   Jeruel: on the west short of the Dead Sea, south of Engedi.

20.20   Tekoa: about 16 kilometers south of Jerusalem.

20.25   One ancient translation cattle; Hebrew among them.

20.26   Beracah Valley: leading down from the highlands of Judah to the Dead Sea, at Engedi.
Beracah: this name in Hebrew means "praise."

20.36   Eziongeber: a port at the northern end of the Gulf of Aqaba.

21.1   David's City: see 5.2.

21.7   He had made a covenant with David: see 1 Kgs 11.36.

21.10   independent of; or in revolt against.
        Libnah: some 20 kilometers west of Jerusalem, near the Philis-
        tine border.

21.16   The coast: of the Mediterranean Sea.

21.20   David's City: see 5.2.

22.2-3 Some ancient translations (and see 2 Kgs 8.26) twenty-two;
        Hebrew forty-two.

22.5   Gilead: on the east side of the Jordan.

22.6   Jezreel: in northern Israel, about 65 kilometers from Ramoth.

22.10   King Ahaziah's mother Athaliah: daughter of King Ahab of Israel
        and widow of King Jehoram of Judah.

23.11   a copy of the laws governing kingship; or royal insignia or
        bracelets.

23.17   Baal: see 17.3.

23.18   Law of Moses: see 17.9.

24.6   Probable text required the people; Hebrew unclear.
        Tent of the LORD's presence: see 1 Chr 6.32.

24.7   that corrupt woman; or whom she had corrupted.
        Baal: see 17.3.

24.16   David's City: see 5.2.

24.18   Asherah: see 14.3.

24.25   Some ancient translations son; Hebrew sons.
        David's City: see 5.2.

25.4   The Law of Moses: see Deut 24.16.

25.8   Some ancient translations You may think that they will make you
        stronger; Hebrew unclear.

25.11   Salt Valley: south of the Dead Sea.

25.12   the cliff at the city of Sela; or a cliff.

25.13   Samaria: the capital of the northern kingdom of Israel; Beth
        Horon was to the south, near the border with the southern kingdom
        of Judah.

25.17   challenging him to fight; or inviting him to a conference.

25.21   Beth Shemesh: some 24 kilometers southwest of Jerusalem.

25.24   Obed Edom: see 1 Chr 13.13-14.

25.27   Lachish: some 35 kilometers southwest of Jerusalem.

25.28   David's City: see 5.2.

26.2   Elath: the port at the northern end of the Gulf of Aqaba.

26.7   Meunites: see 20.1.

27.2   he did not sin by burning incense; or he did not take part in the worship.

27.9   David's City: see 5.2.

28.2   Baal: see 17.3.

28.3   Hinnom Valley: to the south of Jerusalem.

29.3   First month: Abib, the Jewish month that began with the first new moon occurring after the modern March 11.

29.15   Then, as the king...LORD; or Then they began to make the Temple ritually clean, as the king, who was acting at the LORD's command, had ordered them to do.

29.16   Kidron Valley: east of the city.

29.35   The sacrifices which the people ate: known as fellowship offerings.

30.1-3 Passover Festival: held on the 14th day of Nisan (the first month) to commemorate the deliverance of the ancient Hebrews from their slavery in Egypt.
          Second month: Ziv, the Jewish month that began with the first new moon occurring after the modern April 10.

30.13   Festival of Unleavened Bread: held in Nisan 15-22, immediately after Passover (see verse 1), also in commemoration of the deliverance of the ancient Hebrews from their slavery in Egypt. Its name came from the practice of not using leaven (yeast) in making bread during that week.

30.14   Kidron Valley: see 29.16.

30.21   Probable text with all their strength; Hebrew with mighty instruments.

31.1   Asherah: see 14.3.

31.2   Fellowship offerings: see 7.5.

31.3   Law of Moses: see 17.9.

31.5   Gifts...tithes: the gifts were for the priests, and the tithes were for the Levites (see Num 18).

31.7   Third month: Sivan, the Jewish month that began with the first new moon occurring after the modern May 9.

31.16 Probable text thirty; Hebrew three.

32.5   Some ancient translations building towers on it; Hebrew building on the towers.

32.22 Some ancient translations He let the people live in peace; Hebrew He led the people.

32.30 A tunnel: dug through 520 meters (1700 feet) of solid rock, it brought the water down from Gihon Spring (see 1 Kgs 1.33), outside the city walls, to Siloam Pool, inside the city walls.

32.31 The Babylonian ambassadors: see 2 Kgs 20.12-19.

33.3   Baal: see 17.3.
       Asherah: see 14.3.

33.6   Hinnom Valley: see 28.3.
       consulted; or brought back.

33.7   God had said: see 1 Kgs 9.3-5.

33.14 David's City: see 5.2.
       Gihon Spring: outside the city walls, on the east side; it was the principal source of water for Jerusalem.

33.16 Fellowship offerings: see 7.5.

33.18 The prayer he made to his God: perhaps the apocryphal "Prayer of Manasseh" was composed as a result of this statement (see also verse 19, below).

34.3   Asherah: see 14.3.

34.4   Baal: see 17.3.

34.14 The book of the Law: see 17.9.

34.20 Abdon: called Achbor in 2 Kgs 22.12.

34.30 Book of the covenant: see 17.9.

(79)

34.31   Probable text (see 2 Kgs 23.3) by the royal column; Hebrew in his place.

35.1   Passover: see 30.1.
First month: Abib, the Jewish month that began with the first new moon occurring after the modern March 11.

35.3   Teachers: in matters pertaining to the Temple worship.
Covenant Box: see 1 Chr 6.31.

35.4   The responsibilities assigned to you: see 1 Chr 23-26.

35.17   Festival of Unleavened Bread: see 30.13.

35.22   Megiddo: about 40 kilometers southwest of the southern end of Lake Galilee.

35.25   The collection of laments: not the biblical book of Lamentations.

36.4   Changed his name: to show that the king of Judah was subject to the king of Egypt.

36.10   Spring: about March 597 B.C.
Some ancient translations (and see 2 Kgs 24.17) uncle; Hebrew brother.

36.21   The LORD had foretold through...Jeremiah: see Jer 25.11; 29.10.
Sabbath rest: a reference to the requirement of the Law that every seventh year the land was not to be worked (see Lev 25.1-7).

36.22   Emperor: King Cyrus of Persia occupied the city of Babylon in 539 B.C. and began to reign as the emperor of Babylonia.

EZRA

1.1   Emperor: King Cyrus of Persia occupied the city of Babylon in 539 B.C. and began to reign as the emperor of Babylonia.

1.7   The bowls and cups that King Nebuchadnezzar had taken: see 2 Kgs 25.14-15.

1.8   Sheshbazzar: perhaps the same as Shenazzar, the fourth son of King Jehoiachin (see 1 Chr 3.17-18).

2.63   The Jewish governor: Sheshbazzar (see 1.8).
Urim and Thummim: two stones used by the priest to determine God's will; it is not known precisely how they were used.

3.1   Seventh month: Tishri, the Jewish month that began with the first new moon occurring after the modern September 4.

3.2   Instructions written in the Law of Moses: see Exo 27.1-8.

3.3   Even though; or Because.

3.4   Festival of Shelters: see 2 Chr 5.3.

3.7   Tyre and Sidon: Phoenician cities on the Mediterranean coast, north of Palestine.
       Joppa: on the Mediterranean coast, some 60 kilometers from Jerusalem.

3.8   Second month: Ziv, the Jewish month that began with the first new moon occurring after the modern April 10.

3.9   Probable text (see 2.40) Hodaviah; Hebrew Judah.

4.1   Enemies: the people of Samaria.

4.2   Ever since Emperor Esarhaddon...sent us here to live: in 676 B.C.

4.5   Emperor Darius: the account of these events is continued at verse 24. The material in verses 6-23 describes events which took place almost a century later.

4.6   Beginning of the reign of Emperor Xerxes: 485 B.C.

4.7   Reign of Emperor Artaxerxes: from 465 to 424 B.C.
       Bishlam; or with good intent (an expression describing the type of letter written).
       Aramaic: from 4.8 to 6.18 this book is not in Hebrew, but Aramaic, the official language of the Persian Empire.
       The letter...read; or It was in Aramaic and was written in the Aramaic script.

4.8   Rehum, the governor: of Samaria.

4.10   Ashurbanipal: reigned 668-630 B.C.
       West-of-Euphrates Province: under Persian rule the land of Judah was part of this large Persian province west of the Euphrates River.

4.17   Samaria: the name of the former northern kingdom of Israel.

4.24   Second year: 520 B.C.; see footnote at verse 5.

5.1   Haggai and Zechariah: the two prophets whose books in the Bible appear under their names.

5.2   Shealtiel: oldest son of King Jehoiachin (see 1 Chr 3.17).

5.4   Some ancient translations They; Aramaic We.

5.11   A powerful king: Solomon.

5.13   <u>King Cyrus as emperor of Babylonia</u>: see 1.1.

6.2   <u>Ecbatana</u>: the summer residence of the Persian emperors, some 450 kilometers northeast of Babylon.

6.15   <u>Adar</u>: the twelfth Jewish month which began with the first new moon of the modern February.
    <u>Sixth year of the reign of Emperor Darius</u>: about 516 B.C.; so the mention of Artaxerxes (verse 14) is a mistake, since he began to reign some fifty years later (see 4.7; 7.1).

6.19   Beginning with this verse, this book is again in Hebrew (see 4.7).
    <u>Passover</u>: see 2 Chr 30.1.
    <u>First month</u>: Abib, the Jewish month that began with the first new moon occurring after the modern March 11.

6.22   <u>Unleavened Bread</u>: see 2 Chr 30.13.
    <u>Emperor of Assyria</u>: apparently a reference to the Persian emperor who then also ruled the territory once occupied by Assyria, Israel's ancient enemy.

7.1   <u>Artaxerxes</u>: probably Artaxerxes II, emperor of Persia 404-358 B.C.

7.6-7   <u>Seventh year</u>: about 398 B.C.

7.8-9   <u>First month</u>: Abib, the Jewish month that began with the first new moon occurring after the modern March 11.
    <u>Fifth month</u>: Ab, the Jewish month that began with the first new moon occurring after the modern July 7.

7.12   Verses 12-16 are in Aramaic (see also 4.7).
    <u>Aramaic has an additional word, the meaning of which is unclear.</u>

8.2-14   <u>One ancient translation</u> (see also 2.8) Zattu; <u>Hebrew does not have this name.</u>
    <u>One ancient translation</u> (see also 2.10) Bani; <u>Hebrew does not have this name.</u>

8.31   <u>Twelfth day of the first month</u>: see 7.8-9.

9.4   <u>Time for the evening sacrifice</u>: 3:00 P.M.

10.6   <u>One ancient translation</u> spent the night; <u>Hebrew</u> went.

10.9   <u>Ninth month</u>: Kislev, the Jewish month that began with the first new moon occurring in modern November.

10.16   <u>Some ancient translations</u> appointed; <u>Hebrew unclear.</u>
    <u>Tenth month</u>: Tebeth, the Jewish month that began with the first new moon occurring in modern December.

10.44   Verse 44 in Hebrew is unclear.

NEHEMIAH

1.1   Kislev: the ninth Jewish month, which began with the first new moon occurring in modern November.
Twentieth year: about 445 B.C.
Susa: the winter residence of the emperor, in Elam.

1.2   had returned from exile in; or had not been exiled to.

1.3   had survived and...homeland; or had remained in the homeland and had not gone into exile.

2.7   West-of-Euphrates Province: under Persian rule the land of Israel was part of this large Persian province west of the Euphrates River.

2.10   Sanballat: governor of the province of Samaria.
Ammon: on the east side of the Jordan River.

2.15   Kidron Valley: east of the city.

3.1   City wall was rebuilt: according to the following report, the rebuilding of the wall started at the middle of the north side and proceeded counterclockwise around the city. Many of the places mentioned cannot be identified.

3.6   Jeshanah Gate; or the Old Gate.

3.15   David's City: that part of Jerusalem which David had captured from the original inhabitants, the Jebusites (see 2 Sam 5.6-10).

3.16   The pool: a water reservoir.

3.31   Miphkad; or Mustering, or Watch.

4.7   Ashdod: one of the Philistine cities, along the Mediterranean coast.

4.12   Probable text the plans our enemies were making against us; Hebrew unclear.

4.23   Probable text weapons at hand; Hebrew unclear.

5.11   One ancient translation debts; Hebrew unclear.

5.13   Sash: clothing in those days had no pockets, so small items were tucked into the sash that was worn like a belt around the waist. Shaking it out was a symbol of losing everything.

5.14   Twelve years: from 445 to 433 B.C.

5.15   One ancient translation a day; Hebrew unclear.

6.2   Plain of Odo: near Lydda, which was about 40 kilometers northwest of Jerusalem.

6.5   Unsealed letter: leaving a letter unsealed was a deliberate way of making certain that its contents would become widely known.

6.13   Sinning: since Nehemiah was not a priest he would have broken the Law by entering the Holy Place, as Shemaiah had been bribed to suggest (verse 10).

6.15   Elul: the sixth Jewish month, which began with the first new moon after the modern August 6.

7.4   built; or rebuilt.

7.65   The Jewish governor: see Ezra 2.63.
       Urim and Thummim: two stones used by the priest to determine God's will; it is not known precisely how they were used.

8.1   Seventh month: Tishri, the Jewish month that began with the first new moon occurring after the modern September 4.
       The book of the Law: a part, if not all, of the Pentateuch, the first five books of the Old Testament.

8.8   Translation: the Law was written in Hebrew, but in Babylonia the Jews had adopted Aramaic as the language for daily life. Because of this a translation was necessary.
       They gave...explained; or They read God's Law and then translated it, explaining.

8.14   The Law...ordered: see Lev 23.33-43.
       Festival of Shelters: celebrated in the fall after the completion of the harvest. In remembrance of the years when their ancestors wandered through the wilderness, the Israelites constructed rough shelters in which to live during the eight-day celebration. The Jewish name for this festival is Sukkoth (the Hebrew name for "shelters").

8.15   Probable text So they...sent them: Hebrew It also ordered that the following instructions be sent.

9.1-2 Same month: the seventh month (see 8.1).
       Separated themselves from all foreigners: see 13.1-3,23-28.

9.9   Red Sea: (in Hebrew literally "Sea of Reeds") evidently referred originally to (1) a series of lakes and marshes between the head of the Gulf of Suez and the Mediterranean, the region generally regarded as the site of the events described in Exodus 14, and was extended to include (2) the Gulf of Suez, and (3) the Gulf of Aqaba.

10.37 Tithes: one tenth, which by Law belonged to God.

11.8   One ancient translation close relatives; Hebrew after him.

11.14 a member of a leading family; or son of Haggedolim.

11.30 Hinnom Valley: south of Jerusalem.

12.12-21 In Hebrew a name is missing from the list.

12.22 Darius: either Darius II, who ruled 423-404 B.C., or Darius III, 335-331 B.C.

12.24 Probable text (see 10.9 and 12.8) Binnui; Hebrew son of.

12.31 Rubbish Gate: the two groups started somewhere on the south-western part of the city wall and went in opposite directions until they met in front of the Temple in the northeastern part of the city.

12.39 Ephraim Gate, Jeshanah Gate; or Ephraim Gate (also called the Old Gate).

12.44 Tithes: see 10.37.

13.1 Law of Moses: see 8.1.
The passage: see Deut 23.3-5.

13.4 Tobiah: an Ammonite (see 2.10).

13.6 Thirty-second year: about 433 B.C.
Artaxerxes: as emperor of Persia, Artaxerxes also had the title "King of Babylon."

13.16 Tyre: a Phoenician city on the Mediterranean coast, north of Palestine.

13.19 Evening: the Jewish day begins at sunset.
Was over: at sundown of the seventh day (Sabbath).

13.23 Ashdod: see 4.7.

ESTHER

1.1 Susa: the winter residence of the emperor, in Elam.

1.3 Third year: about 483 B.C.

1.8 There were no limits...wanted; or But no one was forced to drink; the king had given orders to the palace servants that everyone could have as much or as little as he wanted.

1.10 Eunuchs: men who had been made physically incapable of having normal sexual relations. They were often important officials in the courts of ancient kings, and the term may have come to be used of such officials in general, regardless of their sexual condition.

1.22 saying; or in order.

2.5   Kish: the father of King Saul (see 1 Sam 9.1-2).

2.6   Exile: in 598 B.C. (see 2 Kgs 24.8-16).

2.14   Concubines: the women who belonged to the royal harem.

2.16   Seventh year: about 478 B.C.
        Tebeth: the Jewish month that began with the first new moon
        occurring in modern December.

2.18   holiday; or remission of taxes.

2.23   hanged on the gallows; or executed by impalement.

3.1   Agag: an Amalekite king (see 1 Sam 15.7-32); his people were
        traditional enemies of the people of Israel.

3.7   Twelfth year: about 472 B.C.
        Nisan: the Jewish month that began with the first new moon
        occurring after the modern March 11.
        Adar: the Jewish month that began with the first new moon
        occurring in modern February.

6.7-8   Ornament: probably a type of crown.

7.4   Sold: a reference to the money Haman had promised the king
        (see 3.9).
        Probable text and not bothered you about it; Hebrew unclear.

7.8   Covered Haman's head: apparently this was done to anyone sentenced
        to die.

7.10   Hanged: see 2.23.

8.3   Agag: see 3.1.

8.9   Sivan: the Jewish month that began with the first new moon
        occurring after the modern May 9.

8.12   The day set: see 3.13.

9.2   In the Jewish quarter of every city; or In every Jewish city;
        or In every city in which Jews lived.

JOB

1.1   Uz: an area whose exact location is unknown; it could have been
        Edom, south of the Dead Sea (see Lam 4.21).
        Who worshiped God: this statement, and those that follow,
        suggest that Job was not Hebrew.

1.3   The East: Palestine and countries east of it.

1.5   Purify: to remove sins; to forgive, pardon.

1.6   Heavenly beings: supernatural beings, either angels or gods, who
serve God in heaven.
       Satan: a supernatural being whose name (Satan means "opponent"
or "accuser") indicates that he was regarded as man's opponent.

1.15   Sabeans: a tribe of wandering raiders from Arabia, to the south.

1.17   Chaldeans: a tribe of wandering raiders from Mesopotamia, to the
north.

1.20   Shaved his head: like the tearing of clothes, a sign of mourning.

2.1   Heavenly beings: see 1.6.
       Satan: see 1.6.

2.7   Sores: some unspecified skin disease; leprosy would be most
unlikely.

2.11   Teman: in Edom, south of the Dead Sea.
       Shuah: perhaps in Mesopotamia or else in northern Arabia.
       Naamah: exact location unknown.

3.8   Sorcerers: magicians who claimed to be able to do such things as
make a day unlucky.
       Leviathan: a legendary sea monster (see Psa 74.14; Isa 27.1),
sometimes identified with the crocodile. Magicians were thought to
be able to command him to make the sun go into eclipse.

3.17   The grave: Sheol, the world of the dead (see 10.21-22).

4.17   righteous in the sight of; or more righteous than.
       be pure before; or be more pure than.

4.18   Heavenly servants: the angels in heaven.

4.19   A creature of clay: a human being (see 10.9).

5.5   Probable text even the grain growing among thorns; Hebrew unclear.

5.7   sparks fly up from a fire; or birds fly up to the sky.

5.15   Probable text poor; Hebrew unclear.

6.4   Shot me with arrows: a figurative way of saying that God sent
disease and suffering on him.

6.7   Probable text sick; Hebrew unclear.

6.14   Probable text trouble; Hebrew unclear. The verse may be translated Whoever refuses to be kind to a friend shows no reverence
for God.

6.19   Sheba and Tema: towns in Arabia which were centers of commerce.

6.21   Probable text like; Hebrew because.
One Hebrew manuscript and some ancient translations to me; most Hebrew manuscripts have nothing in the text and to him in the margin.

7.6   Weaver's shuttle: a small device in the loom which carries threads back and forth rapidly as cloth is being woven.

7.9-10   Never returns: from Sheol, the world of the dead (see 10.21-22).

7.12   Sea monster: a reference to ancient stories in which sea monsters had to be guarded so that they would not escape and do damage.

8.17   Probable text hold fast to; Hebrew see.

9.3   He can ask...answer; or A man could ask him a thousand questions, and he would not answer.

9.6   The pillars that support the earth: it was thought that the surface of the earth was supported by pillars which rested on a solid foundation beneath the seas.

9.8   Trample the sea monster's back: a reference to ancient stories in which a sea monster was killed and then trampled (see also 26.13).

9.9   The Dipper: a group of stars resembling a water dipper, also known as Ursa Major, "Large Bear."
Orion: a group of stars named for the legendary hunter Orion.
Pleiades: a group of stars named for the seven daughters of the legendary hero Atlas.
The stars of the south: a constellation that cannot now be identified.

9.13   Rahab: a legendary sea monster which represented the forces of chaos and evil.

9.19   Probable text make him go; Hebrew make me go.

9.31   A pit with filth: a figure of sin.

10.8   Some ancient translations and now; Hebrew together.

10.9   One ancient translation from clay; Hebrew like clay.

10.15   Probable text covered with shame; Hebrew see my shame.

10.21   A land: Sheol, the world of the dead, which was thought to be a vast abyss in the depths of the earth.

12.4   but there was...prayers; or I prayed to God for help and he punished me.

13.14 <u>One ancient translation</u> I am; <u>Hebrew</u> Why am I.

14.6 <u>One Hebrew manuscript</u> and leave him alone; <u>most Hebrew manu-</u><u>scripts</u> so that he may rest.
<u>let him</u> enjoy his hard life--if he can; <u>or</u> until he finishes his day of hard work.

14.13 <u>World of the dead</u>: see 10.21-22.

15.23 <u>One ancient translation</u> vultures; <u>Hebrew</u> where is he?
<u>One ancient translation</u> are waiting; <u>Hebrew</u> he wanders.

15.29 <u>One ancient translation</u> shadow; <u>Hebrew unclear</u>.

15.30 <u>One ancient translation</u> blossoms; <u>Hebrew</u> mouth.

15.32 <u>Some ancient translations</u> wither; <u>Hebrew</u> be filled.

16.8 <u>Verses 7-8 in Hebrew are unclear</u>.

16.13 <u>Shoots arrows</u>: see 6.4.

16.19 <u>Someone</u>: it is impossible to determine who this is; it can hardly be God himself, for in verse 21 Job wishes that someone would plead with God for him.

17.5 a man...suffer for it; <u>or</u> a man entertains his friends while his children go hungry.

17.13 <u>World of the dead</u>: see 10.21-22.

17.16 <u>One ancient translation</u> with me; <u>Hebrew unclear</u>.

18.5 <u>Light</u>: a figure of health and life.

18.15 <u>Probable text</u> Now anyone may live in his tent; <u>Hebrew unclear</u>.
<u>To disinfect it</u>: sulfur was used in the ancient world as a dis-infectant and to clean rooms that had contained corpses.

18.16 <u>His roots and branches</u>: perhaps a figure of ancestors and descendants.

19.20 <u>Verse 20 in Hebrew is unclear</u>.

19.24 last forever; <u>or</u> be on record.

19.26 while still in this body; <u>or</u> although not in this body.
<u>Verse 26 in Hebrew is unclear</u>.

19.29 one who judges; <u>or</u> a judgment.

20.17 <u>Probable text</u> He will...oil; <u>Hebrew unclear</u>.
<u>Streams that flow</u>: a figure of abundance.

21.17   Light: see 18.5.

21.22   those in high places; or the angels.

22.11   Dark...a flood: figures of suffering and misfortune.

22.14   Dome of the sky: the place on which God was believed to walk to inspect the earth and mankind.

22.23   One ancient translation humbly; Hebrew be built up.

22.29   Probable text proud; Hebrew unclear.

22.30   Some ancient translations innocent; Hebrew not innocent. Verse 30 in Hebrew is unclear.

23.7   he would declare me innocent; or then my rights would be safe.

23.8-9   East...West...North...South: Job had traveled over the whole earth in his search for God.

24.2   Property lines: marked by stones, which were easily moved.

24.6   Fields they don't own: having been cheated out of their own land, the poor are forced to work for others for very small pay.

24.18   Zophar is not named in the text, but this speech is usually assigned to him.

26.5   Bildad is not named in the text, but this speech is usually assigned to him.
The waters under the earth: the great subterranean ocean, here the same as the world of the dead in verse 6.

26.6   World of the dead: see 10.21-22.

26.10   A circle...on the face of the sea: a poetic way of speaking of the horizon, where darkness and light successively give way to each other.

26.11   Pillars: it was thought that the solid sky was supported by pillars which rested on a foundation beneath the seas.

26.12   Conquered the sea: a reference to an ancient story in which the sea fought against God.
Rahab: see 9.13.

26.13   Escaping monster: see 9.8.

27.13   Zophar is not named in the text, but this speech is usually assigned to him.

27.15   Their widows will not mourn: they will not have the chance to observe the proper mourning period (see Psa 78.64).

27.18   Some ancient translations spider's web; Hebrew moth or bird's nest.
Spider's web...hut: both structures are flimsy and temporary; they don't last long.

27.19   Some ancient translations One last time; Hebrew They will not be gathered.

28.1   Section Heading: The Hebrew text does not indicate who is speaking in this chapter.

28.6   Sapphire: a precious stone, usually blue in color.

28.11   Some ancient translations dig to the sources of; Hebrew bind from trickling.

28.18   Coral: a stony substance found in the sea which is used to make jewelry.
Crystal: a semi-precious stone, usually clear and colorless.
Ruby: a precious stone, deep-red in color.

28.19   Topaz: a semi-precious stone, usually yellow in color.

28.22   Destruction: here a name for Sheol, the world of the dead.

29.13   in deepest misery; or about to die.
widows; or their widows.

30.4   Broom tree: its roots have such a bitter taste that they are almost inedible.

30.13   Probable text stop; Hebrew help.

30.24   Verse 24 in Hebrew is unclear.

31.18   Probable text All my life I have taken care of them; Hebrew unclear.

31.33   Other men try to hide their sins; or Adam tried to hide his sin.

32.2   Elihu: because he is not included at the beginning (2.11-13) or end (42.7) of the story, this section (32.1--37.24) may not have been originally a part of the book.

34.1   You men: Job's three friends, Eliphaz, Bildad, and Zophar.

34.23   Probable text a time; Hebrew yet.

36.12   World of the dead: see 10.21-22.

(91)

36.25　but we can only watch from a distance; <u>or</u> no one understands it all.

36.31　<u>Probable text</u> feeds; <u>Hebrew</u> judges.

37.7　<u>One ancient translation</u> them what he can do; <u>Hebrew</u> this to those whom he has made.

37.11　<u>Verse 11 in Hebrew is unclear.</u>

37.18　<u>As hard as polished metal</u>: the sky was thought of as a solid dome (see 22.14; Gen 1.6-8).

38.1　<u>The storm</u>: a frequent setting for God's appearances (see Psa 18. 7-15; 50.3; Ezek 1.4).

38.6　<u>The pillars</u>: see 9.6.

38.7　<u>Heavenly beings</u>: see 1.6.

38.8　<u>Hold back the sea</u>: see 26.12.

38.31　<u>Pleiades...Orion</u>: see 9.9.

38.32　<u>The Big and the Little Dipper</u>: two groups of stars resembling water dippers, also known as <u>Ursa Major</u>, "Large Bear" and <u>Ursa Minor</u>, "Little Bear" (see 9.9).

38.36　<u>Ibis</u>: a bird in ancient Egypt that was believed to announce the flooding of the Nile River.
　　　　<u>Rooster</u>: it was believed that the rooster could predict the coming of rain.
　　　　<u>Verse 36 in Hebrew is unclear.</u>

39.13　<u>Verse 13 in Hebrew is unclear.</u>

39.18　<u>Probable text</u> run; <u>Hebrew unclear.</u>

40.15　<u>Behemoth</u>: identified by some with the hippopotamus, by others with a legendary monster.

40.20　<u>Verse 20 in Hebrew is unclear.</u>

41.1　<u>Leviathan</u>: see 3.8.

41.11　<u>Verse 11 in Hebrew is unclear.</u>

41.13　<u>One ancient translation</u> armor; <u>Hebrew</u> bridle.

41.15　<u>Some ancient translations</u> back; <u>Hebrew</u> pride.

41.25　strongest; <u>or</u> gods.

41.30   Threshing sledge: an implement used to thresh grain, with sharp pieces of iron or stone fastened underneath it.

42.6   Dust and ashes: scattered on the head and body as a sign of mourning or penitence.

42.7   Your two friends: Bildad and Zophar; no account is taken of Elihu (see 32.2).

42.14   In Hebrew the names of Job's daughters suggest beauty both by their sound and by their meaning. JEMIMAH means "dove"; KEZIAH means "cassia," a variety of cinnamon used as a perfume; and KEREN HAPPUCH means a small box in which eye make-up was kept.

PSALMS

Psalm 1   The contrast between the life and destiny of God's faithful people and of those who do not obey him.

1.2   The Law of the LORD: the Torah, the first five books of the Hebrew Scriptures.

1.4   Straw: in the process of winnowing grain, the crushed sheaves were tossed into the air; the grain fell to the ground and the straw was blown away.

1.5   Will be condemned: on the Judgment Day.
Kept apart from God's own people: they will not share in their reward on the Judgment Day.

Psalm 2   At his coronation the king of Israel is promised universal dominion by God. Jews and Christians alike have interpreted this psalm messianically.

2.2   The king he chose: the king of Israel, God's representative on earth.
Verses 1-2 are quoted in Acts 4.25-26 as they appear in the ancient Greek version, the Septuagint.

2.6   Zion: the term Zion (originally a designation for "David's City," the Jebusite stronghold captured by King David's forces) was later extended in meaning to refer to the hill on which the Temple stood.
My king: the king chosen by God (see verse 2).

2.7   My son: see 2 Sam 7.14; Psa 89.26-27.
Today: the day on which the king was crowned.

2.12   Probable text tremble...him; some other possible texts with trembling kiss his feet and with trembling kiss the Son and tremble and kiss the mighty one; Hebrew unclear.

(93)

<u>Psalm 3</u>   A prayer for help by a man, perhaps the king (see verses 3, 6-7), whose life is threatened by enemies.

3.4   <u>Sacred hill</u>: Mount Zion in Jerusalem, which formed part of the Temple and palace area (see 2.6).

3.5   <u>All night long</u>: perhaps this refers to spending the night in the Temple.

<u>Psalm 4</u>   A prayer for help by one who is threatened by enemies.

4.2   <u>What is worthless...what is false</u>: either pagan idols or false accusations against the psalmist.

4.3   <u>The righteous</u>: the psalmist himself.

4.5   <u>Right sacrifices</u>: those required by the Law of Moses.

4.8   <u>I lie down</u>: perhaps to spend the night in the Temple (see 3.5).

<u>Psalm 5</u>   A prayer for help by one who is threatened by enemies.

5.3   <u>Sunrise</u>: perhaps in the Temple, after spending the night there (see 3.5).
prayer; <u>or</u> sacrifice.

<u>Psalm 6</u>   A prayer for help by one who is sick and near death (verses 5-6) and who has many enemies (verses 7-10).

6.1   <u>Angry</u>: sickness was regarded as the result of God's anger because of human sin.

6.2   Give me strength; <u>or</u> Heal me.

6.5   <u>The world of the dead</u>: the destiny of all who die, Sheol, in the depths of the earth, was thought of as a place of darkness, dust, and silence (see Job 3.17-19; Psa 88.10-12).

6.10   <u>Be driven away</u>: God will punish them.

<u>Psalm 7</u>   A prayer by one who is being accused by his enemies of wrong-doing (see verses 3-4) and who asks the LORD to judge in his favor (verses 8-9,17).

Hebrew title: <u>Cush the Benjaminite</u>: no person by this name appears in the Old Testament.

7.3-4   These are the crimes which the psalmist's enemies accuse him of. without cause done violence to my enemy; <u>or</u> shown mercy to someone who wronged me unjustly.

7.7   Probable text rule over them from above; Hebrew return above
over them.
        rule over them; or judge them.

7.15-16   Punished: the teaching that evil people are punished by their
own evil appears often (see 9.15; 35.7-8; 57.6).

7.17   I thank the LORD for his justice: the psalmist is confident that
the LORD will prove him innocent.
        The Most High: a frequently used title of God as the greatest,
the most powerful, of all gods.

Psalm 8   A hymn praising God's greatness and man's God-given dignity.

8.1   LORD...Lord: the first one translates the Hebrew name for the
God of Israel (Yahweh or Jehovah); the second one translates his
title ("master, sovereign").

8.2   The first part of this verse is quoted in Matt 21.16 as it
appears in the ancient Greek version, the Septuagint.

8.3   The sky, which you have made: see Gen 1.6-8.
        The moon and the stars: see Gen 1.16.

8.5   yourself; or the gods; or the angels. The Septuagint translates
"the angels," and it is so quoted in Heb 2.7.

8.6-8   Ruler: for man's role as ruler of all creation see Gen 1.26-28.
In I Cor 15.27 verse 6 is applied to Christ.

Psalm 9   A prayer of thanksgiving for God's help, joined to a plea
that God will punish the psalmist's enemies. Originally Psalms 9
and 10 were one composition (as they are in the Greek and Latin
versions).

9.3   My enemies: the language suggests a battle in which God defeated
the psalmist's enemies (see verses 5-6).

9.11   Zion: the city of Jerusalem.

9.15   See 7.15-16.

9.17   Death: in Hebrew "Sheol," the world of the dead (see 6.5).

Psalm 10   A prayer for help by one who feels oppressed and persecuted.

10.4   God doesn't matter: the wicked man believes that God is not
concerned with human affairs (see verse 11).

10.5   Succeeds: this is the opinion of the wicked man (see verse 6).

10.16   His land: the land of Israel.

Psalm 11 A song of confidence, expressing assurance that God rewards the good and punishes the wicked.

11.1 Some ancient translations like a bird to the mountains; Hebrew bird, to your (plural) mountains.

11.4 Temple: either in heaven (parallel with throne in heaven in the next line) or in Jerusalem.

11.6 One ancient translation coals; Hebrew traps.
Burning sulfur: see the account of the destruction of Sodom and Gomorrah (Gen 19.24-25).

Psalm 12 A prayer for help by the people of Israel, who are distressed by the breakdown of public order and justice.

12.6 Refined seven times: pure silver ore, from which all impurities have been removed.

Psalm 13 A prayer for help by one who is sick and is persecuted by his enemies.

13.4 Downfall: either the psalmist's financial ruin or his death.

Psalm 14 A complaint about widespread evil, joined to a confident hope that God will once again bless his people. This psalm is almost exactly like Psalm 53.

14.1 Fools: those who refuse to acknowledge God and obey his will (see Prov 9.10); in contrast, wise people are those who worship God (see verse 2).
There is no God: not a denial of God's existence but of his interest in human affairs.

14.7 Zion: see 2.6.
makes them prosperous again; or restores them to their homeland.

Psalm 15 A description of the qualities that God requires of those who would worship and serve him.

15.1 Who may enter?: this question is asked by pilgrims seeking admission to worship in the Temple.
Sacred hill: see 2.6.

15.2 The answer (verses 2-5) lists the qualities required of faithful worshipers of God.

15.5 Makes loans: for helping someone in need, not as a business matter; Israelites were forbidden from charging interest on loans to fellow Israelites (see Lev 25.36-37; Deut 23.19-20).

Psalm 16   A song of gratitude to God for his protection and care.

16.2   LORD...Lord: see 8.1.

16.3   How excellent are the LORD's faithful people; or The gods in the
land are powerful.

16.4   Probable text Those...themselves; Hebrew unclear.

16.8-11   These verses are quoted in Acts 2.25-28 as they appear in the
ancient Greek translation, the Septuagint.

16.10   Quoted in Acts 13.35.
The world of the dead: see 6.5.

Psalm 17   A prayer for help by one whose enemies falsely accuse him of
wrongdoing; the psalmist knows that the LORD will prove him innocent.

17.5   Your way: the way that God marks out for his people to follow.

17.8   The shadow of your wings: a figure of God's care and protection
(see Deut 32.10-11).

17.15   Awake: either after spending the night in the Temple (see 3.5) or
coming to life after death.

Psalm 18   A king's song of thanksgiving to God for giving him victory
in battle. This psalm, with a few differences, is found also in
2 Sam 22.2-51.

Hebrew title: see 2 Sam 22.1; for David's escape from Saul, see
1 Sam 23.7-14.

18.5   The grave: Sheol, the world of the dead (see 6.5).

18.6   His temple: God's dwelling in heaven (see verses 10-11).

18.10   His winged creature: the Hebrew "cherub" (plural "cherubim") is
portrayed as a winged animal guarding God's heavenly throne (see
Ezek 1.5-14; 10.21); the cherubim above the Covenant Box in the
Temple represented God's earthly throne (see 2 Sam 6.2; 2 Kgs 19.15).

18.13   The Most High: see 7.17.
One ancient translation (and see 2 Sam 22.14) was heard; Hebrew
was heard hailstones and flashes of fire.

18.15   The foundations of the earth: it was believed that the surface
of the earth was supported by pillars which rested on a foundation
in the depths of the seas (see 24.2).

18.16   The deep waters: a figure of extreme danger (see verse 4).

18.26   hostile; or perverse.

18.28   Light: a figure of life and vitality.

18.35   care; or kindness.

18.43   A rebellious people: the king's own subjects.

Psalm 19   A hymn of praise to God the Creator (verses 1-6) and to the Law of the LORD (verses 7-14).

19.4   Some ancient translations message; Hebrew line.

19.7   The Law of the LORD: see 1.2.

19.13   The evil of sin; or the greatest sin (that is, idolatry).

19.14   Redeemer: when used of a man this term refers to the closest relative who had the duty of providing for someone in need (see Ruth 2.20; 3.12).

Psalm 20   A prayer asking God to give the king victory, probably offered in the Temple before the battle (verses 2-3).

20.2   Mount Zion: see 2.6.

20.9   Some ancient translations answer; Hebrew he will answer.

Psalm 21   A hymn of praise to God for having given the king victory in battle; for this reason this psalm is placed next to Psalm 20 (compare verse 2 with 20.4).

21.10   the king; or the LORD.

Psalm 22   An anguished cry to God for help (verses 1-21), followed by a promise to praise God for answering the psalmist's prayer (verses 22-31).

22.1   My God: these words were quoted by Jesus on the cross (Matt 27.46; Mark 15.34).

22.8   The language of this verse was used by Jesus' opponents at the crucifixion (Matt 27.43).

22.12   Bashan: a territory northeast of Lake Galilee with good grazing fields, and which was famous for its fine cattle.

22.15   Probable text throat; Hebrew strength.

22.16   Some ancient translations they tear at; others they tie; Hebrew like a lion.

22.18   This verse is quoted in John 19.24 (see also Matt 27.35; Mark 15.24; Luke 23.34).
      They gamble: probably by using small marked stones, like dice.

22.21   Some ancient translations I am helpless; Hebrew you answered me.

22.22   Assembly: public worship in the Temple (see verse 25).

22.26   Eat as much as they want: in a fellowship meal following the offering of sacrifices in the Temple (see Lev 3.1-5).

22.29   Probable text will bow down to him; Hebrew will eat and bow down.

22.30   future generations; one Hebrew manuscript has my descendants.

Psalm 23 A song of confidence in the LORD's protection and care.

23.4   Rod: a club used by the shepherd to drive away wild animals.
      Staff: a stout stick used to rescue sheep from dangerous places; the shepherd's crook.

23.6   Your house: the Temple, where God dwells with his people.

Psalm 24 A liturgy used by pilgrims as they arrived in procession at the Temple.

24.2   The deep waters beneath the earth: it was believed that there was a vast ocean under the earth which was the source of rivers and springs.
      Its foundations: see 18.15.

24.3   See 15.1.
      The LORD's hill: the hill in Jerusalem on which the Temple stood (see 2.6).

24.3-6 See 15.2-5.

24.4   worship idols; or love lies.

24.7   The gates: of the Temple in Jerusalem.

Psalm 25 A prayer to God for help.

25.10   Covenant: the pact between God and the people of Israel at Mount Sinai, which the people promised always to keep (see Exo 24.3-8).

25.13   The land: the Promised Land, Canaan, which God gave to his people.

25.21   my goodness and honesty; or your goodness and integrity.

Psalm 26 A prayer for help by one who is accused of wrongdoing and who asks the Lord to prove him innocent.

26.3   your faithfulness always leads me; or I live in loyalty to you.

26.6   March...around your altar: a ritual procession in the Temple.

26.8   The house where you live: the Temple in Jerusalem.
Your glory: the visible manifestation of God's presence and power.

26.12   Assembly: the people of Israel gathered for worship in the Temple (see 22.22).

Psalm 27 A song of confidence (verses 1-6) and a prayer for help (verses 7-14).

27.1   Light: a figure of life and vitality.

27.3   still trust God; or not lose courage.

27.4   The LORD's house: the Temple in Jerusalem (see 23.6).

Psalm 28 A cry to God for protection from personal enemies.

28.1   The world of the dead: see 6.5.

28.2   Lift my hands: in prayer.

28.6-9 Thanksgiving to God for having answered the psalmist's plea.

28.8   king; or people.

Psalm 29 A hymn in praise of God's power manifested in a storm.

29.1   heavenly beings; or gods.

29.2   when he appears; or in garments of worship; or in his beautiful Temple.

29.3   The ocean: the Mediterranean Sea.

29.5   Cedars of Lebanon: famous for their stately beauty and size.

29.6   Mount Hermon: the highest mountain in Syria.

29.8   Kadesh: perhaps the place south of Palestine through which the Israelites passed on their way to Canaan (see Num 20), or else a place in Syria.

29.9   Probable text shakes the oaks; Hebrew makes the deer give birth. Temple: either in heaven or in Jerusalem.

29.10   The deep waters: either the waters above the firmament (Gen 1. 6-7), or else the Flood (Gen 7-8).

Psalm 30 A song of thanksgiving by one who has been saved from death by the LORD.

30.3   The depths below: Sheol, the world of the dead (see 6.5).

30.9   Dead people: in Sheol, the world of the dead, God is not praised (see 6.5).

Psalm 31 A prayer for help by one whose life is threatened by enemies.

31.5   The first part of this verse was quoted by Jesus (Luke 23.46).

31.6   You hate; most Hebrew manuscripts have I hate.

31.10   Some ancient translations troubles; Hebrew iniquity.

31.11   Are afraid of me: perhaps because the psalmist suffered from a loathsome disease.

31.17   The world of the dead: see 6.5.

Psalm 32 A prayer of thanksgiving by one who has been forgiven and healed by God.

32.4   You punished me: probably with a disease, which was taken to be God's punishment for sin.

32.6   Some ancient translations need; Hebrew finding only.

Psalm 33 A hymn of praise to God as creator of the universe and ruler of mankind.

33.2   Harps...stringed instruments: two different musical instruments, a small one, with two to four strings, and a larger one, with ten strings; often translated "harps and lyres."

33.6   See the account of creation in Gen 1.1-19.

33.7   One place...storerooms: the places where the waters above and below the firmament were kept (see Gen 1.6-7). The waters above were the source of rain, and the waters below were the source of rivers and springs.

Psalm 34 A hymn of thanksgiving to God for his protection and care.

Hebrew title: see the account in 1 Sam 21.10--22.1 about David and Achish, king of the Philistine city of Gath.

34.7   His angel: see in Exo 23.20 God's promise to send his angel to protect his people.

34.14   Peace: not just the end of strife but physical and spiritual harmony and well-being.

Psalm 35 A prayer for help by one whose life is threatened by enemies.

35.2-3 God is pictured as a warrior, with his weapons, ready to defend the psalmist.

35.5 Straw: see 1.4.
Angel of the LORD: see 34.7.

35.16 Probable text Like...cripple; one ancient translation They made me suffer and jeered at me; Hebrew unclear.

35.18 Assembly: see 26.12.

35.21 We saw what you did: a false accusation of wrongdoing.

Psalm 36 A meditation on the wickedness of man and the goodness of God.

36.7 precious, O God, is...find; or precious is your constant love! Gods and men find.
The shadow of your wings: see 17.8.

36.9 Light: see 27.1.

Psalm 37 A poem that teaches its readers moral and spiritual truths.

37.3 The land: Israel, the Promised Land (also verses 9,11,22,29,34).

37.11 See Matt 5.5.

37.22 Blessed...cursed: the objects of the LORD's favor and of his anger.

37.35 One ancient translation like a cedar of Lebanon; Hebrew unclear.
Cedar of Lebanon: see 29.5.

Psalm 38 A prayer by a sick man who asks the LORD for forgiveness and healing.

38.1 Punish: disease was seen as God's punishment for sin (see verse 3).

38.5 Foolish: not simply stupid but sinful, which is the cause of his illness.
Sores: some sort of skin disease, resembling leprosy.

38.11 See 31.11.

38.20 are against; or slander.

Psalm 39 A prayer by a sick man who asks the LORD to relent and stop punishing him.

39.8 Save me: heal the disease that has been caused by sin.

39.10 Punish: see 38.1.

39.12 Your guest: this world is seen as God's residence, God's land, in which man lives only for a short time before he leaves (see 1 Chr 29.15).

39.13 Go away: to Sheol, the world of the dead (see 6.5).

Psalm 40 A song of thanksgiving, followed by the psalmist's prayer to God for help against his enemies.

40.2 Pit...quicksand: figures of imminent death.

40.3 This: the psalmist's public confession of God's help.

40.6-8 These verses are quoted in Heb 10.5-7 as they appear in the ancient Greek translation, the Septuagint.

40.6 Ears: the ability to understand and obey God's commands.

40.7 your instructions...Law; or my devotion to you is recorded in your book.

40.9 Assembly: see 26.12.

40.12 No longer see: because of the weeping caused by his suffering (see 6.7).

Psalm 41 A prayer for help by one who is sick and has been forsaken by friends.

41.5 be forgotten; or leave no descendants.

41.7 imagine the worst about; or make evil plans to harm.

41.9 See John 13.18.

41.13 Not a part of the psalm, but the closing doxology of Book One (Psalms 1-41).

Psalm 42 The lament of an Israelite in exile who longs to be back in Jerusalem.

42.2 In your presence: in the Temple in Jerusalem, God's home with his people.

42.3 Where is your God?: God seems to have forgotten the psalmist.

42.6 Mount Hermon: see 29.6.
Mount Mizar: as yet unidentified; perhaps one of the peaks of the Hermon range.

Psalm 43   Originally a part of the preceding psalm.

43.3   Sacred hill: see 2.6.

43.4   Harp: see 33.2.

Psalm 44   A prayer for help by the people of Israel after a military defeat.

44.2   The heathen: the original inhabitants of Canaan, the Promised Land.

44.4   Some ancient translations and my God; you give; Hebrew O God, give.

44.12   as...value; or and made no profit from the sale.

44.13   Our neighbors: nearby countries.

44.17   Covenant: see 25.10.

44.19   Wild animals...deepest darkness: figures of danger and death in foreign countries.

Psalm 45   A song composed for the king's wedding to a foreign princess.

45.4   Probable text and justice; Hebrew and meekness of justice.

45.6   The kingdom that God has given you; or Your kingdom, O God; or Your divine kingdom.

45.8   Myrrh and aloes: plants whose resin was used as perfume.

45.12   Tyre: a Phoenician city on the Mediterranean coast.

45.16   the whole earth; or all the land.

Psalm 46   A hymn in praise of God's power and his care for his people.

46.4   The city of God: Jerusalem.
       The sacred house: the Temple in Jerusalem.
       The Most High: see 7.17.

Psalm 47   A hymn in praise of God's power as king of all the earth.

47.2   The Most High: see 7.17.

47.9   Probable text with the people; Hebrew the people.

Psalm 48   A hymn in praise of Jerusalem, the earthly home of God.

48.1   Sacred hill: see 2.6.

Psalm 49   A meditation on the folly of trusting in riches.

49.7   himself; some Hebrew manuscripts have his fellow man.

49.11   Some ancient translations graves; Hebrew inner thoughts.

49.13   One ancient translation the fate of those; Hebrew after them.

49.14   Probable text far from their homes; Hebrew unclear.
The world of the dead: Sheol (see 6.5).

49.20   cannot keep him from death; some Hebrew manuscripts have keeps
him from understanding.

Psalm 50   In praise of God, the judge of all mankind.

50.2   Zion: Jerusalem (see 2.6).

50.14   Let the giving...to God; or Offer your thanksgiving sacrifice
to God.

50.16   Covenant: see 25.10.

Psalm 51   A confession of sin and a plea for forgiveness.

Hebrew title: see 2 Sam 11.1--12.15.

51.4   The second part of this verse is quoted in Rom 3.4 as it appears
in the ancient Greek translation, the Septuagint.

51.11   Your holy spirit: the divine power that sustains life and joy.

51.14   Spare my life...me; or O God my savior, keep me from the crime
of murder.
righteousness; or saving power.

Psalm 52   The doom that awaits those who trust in their power and wealth.

Hebrew title: see 1 Sam 21.7; 22.9-10.

52.8   Like an olive tree: a figure of prosperity and security.
The house of God: the Temple in Jerusalem.

Psalm 53   A complaint about widespread evil, joined to a confident hope
that God will once again bless his people (see Psalm 14).

53.1   Fools: see 14.1.
There is no God: see 14.1.

53.6   Zion: see 2.6.
makes them prosperous again; or restores them to their homeland.

<u>Psalm 54</u> A prayer for help by one whose life is threatened by enemies.

  <u>Hebrew title</u>: see 1 Sam 23.15-24; 26.1-5.

54.3   Proud men; <u>some Hebrew manuscripts have</u> Foreigners.

54.6   I will gladly offer you a sacrifice; <u>or</u> I will offer you a free-will offering.

<u>Psalm 55</u> A prayer for help by one who is threatened by enemies and has been abandoned by friends.

55.15 <u>Go down alive</u>: see Num 16.31-33.
       <u>The world of the dead</u>: Sheol (see 6.5).

55.17 <u>Morning, noon, and night</u>: the regular hours for prayer.

<u>Psalm 56</u> A prayer for help by one whose life is threatened by enemies.

  <u>Hebrew title</u>: see 1 Sam 21.10-15; 27.1-4.

56.7   <u>Probable text</u> Punish; <u>Hebrew</u> Save.

56.8   <u>Your book</u>: see Exo 32.32-33.

56.9   I know this: God; <u>or</u> Because I know that God.

<u>Psalm 57</u> A prayer for help by one whose life is threatened by enemies.

  <u>Hebrew title</u>: see 1 Sam 24.

57.1   <u>Shadow of your wings</u>: see 17.8.
       <u>Raging storms</u>: a figure of danger.

57.2   <u>The Most High</u>: see 7.17.

57.7-11 See 108.1-5.

57.8   <u>Harp and lyre</u>: see 33.2.

<u>Psalm 58</u> A prayer asking God to destroy the people's enemies.

58.1   rulers; <u>or</u> gods.

58.7   <u>Probable text</u> may...path; <u>Hebrew unclear</u>.

58.8   <u>Snails that dissolve into slime</u>: from the trail of slime left by snails it was thought they dissolved, leaving only their empty shells.

58.9   <u>Verse 9 in Hebrew is unclear</u>.

Psalm 59   A prayer for help against personal enemies and the enemies
      of Israel.

      Hebrew title: see 1 Sam 19.11-17.

59.11   Do not kill them; or Surely you will kill them?
      My people: the psalmist may be the king.

Psalm 60   A prayer for help by the people of Israel after a military
      defeat.

      Hebrew title: see 2 Sam 8.3-8,13; 1 Chr 18.3-12.

60.1   angry with us...us; or angry with us and turned your back on us.

60.5-12   See 108.6-13.

60.6   From his sanctuary; or In his holiness.
      Shechem: an ancient city some 50 kilometers north of Jerusalem.
      Sukkoth Valley: on the east side of the Jordan River.

60.7   Gilead: a country east of the Jordan.
      Manasseh...Ephraim...Judah: three of the tribes of Israel.

60.8   Moab: a country east of the Dead Sea.
      Edom: a country south of the Dead Sea.
      Philistines: a people whose country was on the Mediterranean
      coast.

60.9   Me: the psalmist may be the king.
      The fortified city: probably Sela, the capital of Edom.

Psalm 61   A prayer by one who in exile longs to be back in Jerusalem.

61.4   Your sanctuary: the Temple in Jerusalem.
      Your wings: see 17.8. Here the allusion may be to the Covenant
      Box, in the Most Holy Place, which had on its top figures of winged
      animals, God's earthly throne (see 18.10).

Psalm 62   A song of trust in God's protection and care.

62.3   A man: a reference to the psalmist himself.

62.8   My people: the psalmist may be the king.

Psalm 63   A song of intense longing for God by one who knows that God
      will defeat his enemies.

63.2   The sanctuary: the Temple in Jerusalem.

63.7   The shadow of your wings: see 17.8.

63.9   The world of the dead: Sheol (see 6.5).

<u>Psalm 64</u>   A prayer by one who knows that God will save him from his enemies.

64.3   <u>Cruel words</u>: either slander and lies or else magical curses which were thought to bring disease or death on the victim.

64.8   <u>Probable text</u> He will destroy them because of those words; Hebrew They will destroy him, those words are against them. <u>Shake their heads</u>: an expression of scorn.

<u>Psalm 65</u>   A prayer of thanksgiving for an abundant harvest.

65.1   <u>Zion</u>: Jerusalem.

65.3   <u>One ancient translation</u> us; <u>Hebrew</u> me.

65.4   <u>Sanctuary</u>: the Temple in Jerusalem.

<u>Psalm 66</u>   A hymn of thanksgiving to God for his protection and care.

66.6   See Exo 14.20-22; Josh 3.14-17.

66.12   <u>Fire and flood</u>: figures of hardships and danger. <u>Some ancient translations</u> safety; <u>Hebrew</u> overflowing.

66.13   <u>Your house</u>: the Temple in Jerusalem.

66.18   ignored my sins; <u>or</u> cherished evil thoughts.

<u>Psalm 67</u>   A prayer of thanksgiving for an abundant harvest.

<u>Psalm 68</u>   A hymn praising God for protecting and guiding his people.

68.4   on the clouds; <u>or</u> across the desert.

68.7   <u>When you led your people</u>: a reference to the departure of the Israelites from Egypt.

68.8   <u>God of Sinai</u>: as the people of Israel went from Egypt to Canaan, God revealed himself to them at Mount Sinai (see Exo 19.16-25).

68.9   <u>Your worn-out land</u>: Canaan, the Promised Land.

68.14   <u>Mount Zalmon</u>: perhaps a mountain about 12 kilometers southeast of the city of Samaria.

68.15   <u>Bashan</u>: a region northeast of Lake Galilee.

68.16   <u>The mountain</u>: Mount Zion, in Jerusalem (see 2.6).

68.17   <u>Probable text</u> comes from Sinai; <u>Hebrew</u> in them, Sinai. <u>The holy place</u>: the Temple in Jerusalem.

68.18   The heights: probably Mount Zion.

68.24   His sanctuary: the Temple in Jerusalem.

68.25   Tambourines: small hand drums, usually played by young women.

68.27   Benjamin...Judah: two tribes in the southern part of the
country.
Zebulun and Naphtali: two tribes in the northern part of the
country.

68.30   Verse 30 in Hebrew is unclear.

68.31   Some ancient translations Ambassadors; Hebrew unclear.

Psalm 69   A prayer for help by one who is sick, abandoned by his family,
and persecuted by his enemies.

69.1   The water: a figure of extreme danger; also deep mud, deep
water, and waves in verse 2 (see also verses 14-15).

69.4   My enemies...they are; or My enemies, who have no reason to hate
me, are.

69.10   Some ancient translations humble myself; Hebrew cry.

69.23   Part of verses 22-23 is quoted in Rom 11.9-10 as it appears in
the ancient Greek translation, the Septuagint.

69.26   those whom; or the one.
those; one manuscript has the one.

69.28   The book of the living: see Exo 32.32-33.

Psalm 70   A prayer for help by one whose life is threatened by enemies.
This psalm is almost completely identical with 40.13-17.

Psalm 71   A prayer by an old man who asks God to save him from his
enemies.

71.3   One ancient translation a strong fortress; Hebrew to go always
you commanded.

71.6   Some ancient translations protected; Hebrew unclear.

71.7   an example; or a warning.

71.22   Harp: see 33.2.

Psalm 72   A prayer for the king at the time of his coronation.

72.5   Hebrew May your people worship you; one ancient translation May
the king live.

72.8   From sea to sea: perhaps from the Mediterranean Sea to the Persian Gulf.

72.10   The islands: in the Mediterranean Sea.

72.17   as he has blessed the king; or and may they wish happiness for the king.

72.18-19   The concluding doxology of Book Two (Psalms 42-72).

72.20   The closing line of an early collection of David's psalms.

Psalm 73   A meditation on God's justice by one who is troubled over the prosperity of the wicked.

73.1   to Israel; or to the upright.

73.7   Some ancient translations their hearts pour out evil; Hebrew unclear.

73.10   Verse 10 in Hebrew is unclear.

73.11   The Most High: see 7.17.

73.14   Punished: probably a reference to illness (see 38.1).

Psalm 74   A prayer by the people, asking God to save them from their victorious enemies.

74.2   Slavery: in Egypt.
        Mount Zion: see 2.6.

74.5   Verse 5 in Hebrew is unclear.

74.9   Sacred symbols: perhaps religious festivals and rituals, or miracles, or symbolic actions performed by prophets.

74.11   Probable text Why do you keep your hands behind you?; Hebrew unclear.

74.13-17   This account of creation employs figurative language used in creation stories of other cultures.

74.14   Leviathan: a legendary monster which was a symbol of the forces of chaos and evil.
        animals; or people.

74.19   your helpless people; one Hebrew manuscript has those who praise you.

74.20   Covenant: see 25.10.

Psalm 75   A national hymn of thanksgiving to God for his care for his people.

75.2   Some ancient translations We proclaim how great you are and tell of; Hebrew Your name is near and they tell of.

75.3   Its foundations: see 18.15.

75.6   Probable text from the north or from the south; Hebrew from the wilderness of the mountains.

75.8   A cup: a figure of divine punishment (see similar language in 60.3).

Psalm 76   A national hymn of thanksgiving to God for having defeated Israel's enemies.

76.2   Mount Zion: see 2.6.

76.10   Verse 10 in Hebrew is unclear.

Psalm 77   A prayer on behalf of the nation, in which the psalmist recalls God's care in the past.

77.1   and he hears me; or so that he will hear me.

77.6   Some ancient translations deep thought; Hebrew song.

77.10   Verse 10 in Hebrew is unclear.
is no longer powerful; or no longer comes to our aid.

77.13   Is holy: is in keeping with God's nature as the Holy One.

77.16   The waters: either the primeval ocean at creation (see 74.13-14) or the sea which the Israelites crossed as they departed from Egypt.

Psalm 78   A meditation on Israel's history in which God's faithfulness and his people's unfaithfulness are repeatedly demonstrated.

78.5-6   See Deut 6.6-7.

78.9   Ephraimites: members of the northern tribe of Ephraim (see verse 67).

78.10   Covenant: see 25.10.

78.12   Miracles: the plagues (see verses 43-51).
Zoan: usually identified as the city of Rameses (see Exo 1.11).

78.13   See Exo 14.21-29.

78.14   See Exo 13.21-22.

78.15-16   See Exo 17.6; Num 20.10-13.

78.17   The Most High: see 7.17.

78.18-31   See Exo 16.2-15; Num 11.4-23,31-35.

78.21   See Num 11.1-3.

78.44-51   See Exo 7.14--12.32.

78.48   hail...lightning; or terrible disease...deadly plague.

78.55   The inhabitants: see Deut 7.1.

78.60   His tent: the place of worship.
Shiloh: the central place of worship, some 32 kilometers north of Jerusalem, for the people of Israel before the time of King David (see Josh 18.1; 1 Sam 1.3).

78.61   See 1 Sam 4.1-22.

78.67   The descendants of Joseph...the tribe of Ephraim: the northern kingdom of Israel.

78.68   The tribe of Judah: the southern kingdom.
Mount Zion: see 2.6.

Psalm 79   A prayer by the people, asking God to rescue them from their victorious enemies (see Psalm 74).

79.5   Angry: the victory of the enemies is seen as the result of God's judgment on his people.

Psalm 80   A prayer by the people, asking God to restore them to their homeland.

80.1   Winged creatures: see 18.10.

80.2   Ephraim...Manasseh: the two most important northern tribes; the tribe of Benjamin was often associated with them.

80.4   Angry: see 79.5.

80.8   A grapevine: a figure for the people of Israel.

80.13   Wild hogs...wild animals: figures for the enemies of Israel.

80.14   Turn to us; or Relent.

Psalm 81   A song to be used at a Temple festival, together with a message from God for his people.

81.2   Tambourines: see 68.25.
        Harps and lyres: see 33.2.

81.3   The festival: probably the Festival of Shelters (see Lev 23.
        33-43).

81.5   when he attacked the land of Egypt; or when they came out of
        Egypt.

81.6   Burdens...loads of bricks: references to slavery in Egypt.

81.7   Meribah: see Exo 17.1-7; Num 20.2-13.

Psalm 82   In praise of God, the supreme ruler of the universe.

82.1   The assembly of the gods: see 89.5-7; Job 1.6; 2.1.

82.6   Sons of the Most High: not as God's offspring but as having
        divine status.

Psalm 83   A prayer asking God to protect his people from foreign
        enemies.

83.6   Edom: a country south of the Dead Sea.
        Ishmaelites: descendants of Ishmael, son of Abraham and Hagar
        (see Gen 25.12-18).
        Moab: on the east side of the Dead Sea.
        Hagrites: a nomadic tribe, living on the east side of the
        Jordan River (see 1 Chr 5.10).

83.7   Gebal: perhaps a region south of the Dead Sea.
        Ammon: on the east side of the Jordan, north of Moab.
        Amalek: a nomadic tribe, living south of Judah.
        Philistia: a country along the Mediterranean coast.
        Tyre: a Phoenician city on the Mediterranean coast, north of
        Palestine.

83.9   The Midianites: see Judges 6-8.
        Sisera and Jabin: see Judges 4.1-24.

83.11   Oreb and Zeeb: see Judges 7.25.
        Zebah and Zalmunna: see Judges 8.21.

Psalm 84   A hymn in praise of the Temple.

84.5   Mount Zion: see 2.6.

84.6   Valley of Baca: location unknown; Baca means "balsam tree."
        pools; or blessings.

(113)

Psalm 85   A prayer on behalf of the people during a time of trouble
          and distress.

85.3   Angry: see 79.5.

85.8   Foolish ways: disobedience to God's laws.

Psalm 86   A prayer for help by one whose life is threatened by enemies.

Psalm 87   A hymn in praise of Jerusalem, where God will be worshiped
          by all peoples.

87.1   Sacred hill: see 2.6.

87.4   Philistia, Tyre: see 83.7.
        Sudan: a country south of Egypt.

Psalm 88   A prayer of despair by one who feels completely abandoned
          by God.

88.4   all my strength is gone; or there is no help for me.

88.6   Pit: Sheol, the world of the dead (see 6.5).

88.7   Your anger: see 79.5.

88.8   Repulsive: probably on account of his sickness (see 31.11).

88.9   every day; or all day long.

88.11-12   A description of Sheol, the world of the dead.

88.15   Probable text I am worn out; Hebrew unclear.

Psalm 89   A composition in which several themes are joined together
          (see the section headings).

89.4   See 2 Sam 7.16.

89.6-7   Heavenly beings...holy ones: the gods who comprise the heavenly
        court over which God rules (see 82.1).

89.10   Rahab: a legendary sea monster which represented the forces of
        chaos and evil.

89.12   Mount Tabor: west of the south end of Lake Galilee.
        Mount Hermon: see 42.6-7.

89.20   See 1 Sam 16.1-13.

89.25   See 80.11.

89.27   My first-born son: see 2.7.

89.40   His city: Jerusalem, the capital city.

89.44   Probable text royal scepter; Hebrew purity.

89.50   I, your servant, am; some Hebrew manuscripts have your servants are.
        Probable text curses; Hebrew crowds.

89.52   The closing doxology of Book Three (Psalms 73-89).

Psalm 90   A meditation on human existence in light of God's eternity, joined to a prayer on behalf of the nation.

90.1   home; some Hebrew manuscripts have refuge.

90.3   Dust: see Gen 3.19.

90.12   Become wise: have the proper reverence for God and obey him.

90.13   Anger: see 79.5.

Psalm 91   A meditation on the security enjoyed by those who trust in God.

91.4   His wings: see 17.8.

91.9   The Most High: see 7.17.
        Probable text your; Hebrew my.

91.11-12   See Matt 4.6; Luke 4.10-11.

91.11   His angels: see 34.7.

91.13   Lions and snakes: figures of enemies and other dangers (see Luke 10.19).

Psalm 92   A hymn of praise to God for his protection and care.

92.3   Stringed instruments...harp: see 33.2.

92.10   happiness; or success.

92.12   Cedars of Lebanon: see 29.5.

Psalm 93   A hymn of praise to God as king.

93.3-4 At creation God overcame the chaos and subdued it (see 74.13-17; 89.9-10).

Psalm 94   A prayer asking God to punish the wicked, who oppress the
    people.

94.17   The land of silence: Sheol, the world of the dead (see 6.5).

Psalm 95   A hymn calling on the people to praise God as king.

95.8   Meribah...Massah: see Exo 17.1-7; Num 20.1-13.

95.10   Forty years: see Num 14.33-34.

95.11   See Deut 12.9-10.

Psalm 96   A hymn calling on all people to praise God as king.

96.9   when he appears; or in garments of worship; or in his beautiful
    Temple.

Psalm 97   In praise of God as king of all the earth.

97.5   LORD...Lord: see 8.1.

97.7   all the gods bow down; or bow down, all gods.

97.8   Zion: Jerusalem.

97.10   Probable text The LORD loves those who hate evil; Hebrew Hate
    evil, you who love the LORD.

97.11   Light: a figure of life and vitality.

Psalm 98   A hymn in praise of God as king.

98.5   Harps: see 33.2.

Psalm 99   A hymn in praise of God as king.

99.1   Winged creatures: see 18.10.

99.2   Zion: Jerusalem.

99.4   Probable text Mighty king; Hebrew The might of the king.

99.5   His throne: the Covenant Box in the Most Holy Place of the Temple.

99.9   Sacred hill: see 2.6.

Psalm 100   A hymn of praise to God.

100.2   Before him: in public worship in the Temple.

Psalm 101   A royal psalm, in which the king promises to be an honest
   and just ruler.

101.2   When will you come to me?: an expression of the king's hope that
   God will reveal his will and power.

101.4   not be dishonest; or stay away from dishonest people.
   evil; or evil men.

101.8   The city of the LORD: Jerusalem.

Psalm 102   A prayer for help by a young man who is sick and persecuted
   by his enemies; he prays for himself and for Jerusalem.

102.8   Use my name in cursing: they call down on others the same mis-
   fortunes that have come on the psalmist.

102.9-10   Your anger and fury: see 79.5.

102.11   Like the evening shadows: drawing to its close.

102.13   Zion: Jerusalem.

102.25-27   These verses are quoted in Heb 1.10-12 as they appear in
   the ancient Greek translation, the Septuagint.

Psalm 103   A hymn of thanksgiving to God for his love and care.

103.5   Probable text my life; Hebrew unclear.

103.14   Dust: see Gen 3.19.

103.15-16   See 90.5-6.

103.18   Covenant: see 25.10.

Psalm 104   A hymn of praise to God as creator and sustainer of the
   universe.

104.3   The waters above: a reference to the waters above the celestial
   dome (see Gen 1.6-7).

104.4   This verse is quoted in Heb 1.7 as it appears in the ancient
   Greek translation, the Septuagint.

104.5   Its foundations: see 18.15.

104.16   Cedars of Lebanon: see 29.5.

104.26   Leviathan: see 74.14.
   in it plays...made; or Leviathan is there, that sea monster you
   made to amuse you.

(117)

104.30 give them breath; or send out your spirit.

Psalm 105 A hymn of praise to God as savior and protector of his people.

105.5-6 the man he chose; some Hebrew manuscripts have the people he chose.

105.7-11 God's covenant with Abraham, Isaac, and Jacob.

105.8 Covenant: see 25.10.

105.12-15 The period of the patriarchs.

105.15 My prophets: here the Hebrew patriarchs (see Gen 20.7).

105.16-22 Joseph in Egypt.

105.16 Their country: Canaan, where Jacob and his family were living.

105.19 proved him right; or put him to the test.

105.26-36 The Israelites are set free from Egypt.

105.28 Some ancient translations did not obey; Hebrew obeyed.

105.37-45 From Egypt to the Promised Land.

105.40 Some ancient translations They; Hebrew He.

Psalm 106 A confession of Israel's constant rebellion against God, who is always faithful in keeping his promise.

106.7 Probable text the Almighty; Hebrew the sea.
       The Red Sea: (in Hebrew literally "Sea of Reeds") evidently referred originally to (1) a series of lakes and marshes between the head of the Gulf of Suez and the Mediterranean, the region generally regarded as the site of the events described in Exodus 14, and was extended to include (2) the Gulf of Suez, and (3) the Gulf of Aqaba.

106.28 Peor: a mountain in Moab, east of the Jordan River (see Num 25.1-13).
        Baal: a Canaanite god of fertility.

106.32 Meribah: see Exo 17.1-7; Num 20.2-13.
        Moses was in trouble: he was not allowed to enter the Promised Land (see Num 20.12).

106.45 Covenant: see 25.10.

106.47 The people, in exile in Babylonia, pray to be taken back to Israel.

106.48 The closing doxology of Book Four (Psalms 90-106).

Psalm 107   A hymn of praise to God by the people as they come to worship in the Temple.

107.3   Probable text south; Hebrew the Mediterranean Sea (meaning "west").

107.4   a city to live in; or an inhabited city.

107.32 Assembly: see 26.12.

Psalm 108   A prayer asking God to give his people victory over their enemies; the psalm is composed of 57.7-11 and 60.5-12.

108.2   Harp and lyre: see 33.2.

108.7   From his sanctuary; or In his holiness.
        Shechem: an ancient city some 50 kilometers north of Jerusalem.
        Sukkoth Valley: on the east side of the Jordan River.

108.8   Gilead: a country east of the Jordan.
        Manasseh...Ephraim...Judah: three of the tribes of Israel.

108.9   Moab: a country east of the Dead Sea.
        Edom: a country south of the Dead Sea.
        Philistines: a people whose country was on the Mediterranean coast.

108.10 Me: the psalmist may be the king.
        The fortified city: probably Sela, the capital of Edom.

Psalm 109   A prayer by one whose life is threatened by enemies.

109.4   Probable text have prayed for them; Hebrew unclear.

109.8   The second line of this verse, as it appears in the Septuagint, is applied in Acts 1.20 to Judas Iscariot.

109.10 One ancient translation be driven from; Hebrew seek.

109.15 but may they themselves be completely forgotten; some Hebrew manuscripts have may he wipe out all remembrance of them.

109.28 One ancient translation May my persecutors be defeated; Hebrew They persecuted me and were defeated.

109.30 Assembly: see 26.12.

Psalm 110   In honor of the king, on the day of his coronation.

110.1   Right side: the place of honor.
        until; or while.

110.2   Zion: Jerusalem.

110.3   Verse 3 in Hebrew is unclear.

110.4   in the priestly order of Melchizedek; or like Melchizedek; or
in the line of succession to Melchizedek.
Melchizedek: king of Jerusalem and a priest, who blessed Abraham
(see Gen 14.18-20).

Psalm 111   In praise of God for his love and care.

111.1   Assembly: see 26.12.

111.5   Covenant: see 25.10.

111.8   they were given; or they are to be obeyed.

111.10 The way...the LORD; or The most important part of wisdom is
having reverence for the LORD.

Psalm 112   A meditation on the rewards of obeying God's laws.

112.7   receiving bad news; or hearing vicious rumors.

112.9   See 2 Cor 9.9.

Psalm 113   A hymn in praise to God for his protection and care.

113.3   From the east to the west; or From morning till night.

113.9   Childless wife: such a woman was considered to be punished by
God.

Psalm 114   In praise of God for having freed his people from slavery
in Egypt.

114.3   Red Sea: see 106.7.
The Jordan River stopped flowing: see Josh 3.7-17.

114.4   Skipped...jumped: in fear at the Lord's presence (see Exo 19.18;
Judges 5.5; Psa 68.8).

Psalm 115   In praise of the greatness of the LORD, the one true God.

115.8   May all...become; or All who made them and who trust in them
will become.

115.17 Land of silence: Sheol, the world of the dead (see 6.5).

Psalm 116   A prayer of thanksgiving to God for having saved the psalmist
from death.

116.10 The first part of this verse is quoted in 2 Cor 4.13 as it appears in the ancient Greek translation, the Septuagint.

116.14 Assembly: see 26.12.

Psalm 117 A call for all people to praise the LORD.

Psalm 118 A hymn of thanksgiving to God for having given his people victory over their enemies.

118.5 I: the psalmist is probably the king.

118.10 Many enemies: foreign armies.

118.22-23 See Matt 21.42; Mark 12.10-11.

118.27 The festival: a procession in the Temple.

Psalm 119 In praise of the Law of God. An acrostic poem. In each of the 22 stanzas every one of the 8 verses begins with the same letter of the Hebrew alphabet, from the first letter (aleph) in the first stanza to the last letter (tau) in the twenty-second stanza.

119.1 The law of the LORD: see 1.2.

119.27 teachings; or deeds.

119.37 be good to me, as you have promised; some manuscripts have give me life as I walk in your ways.

119.57 want; or need.

119.66 I trust in; or I believe.

119.73 keep me safe; or fashioned me.

119.74 When they see me: that is, when they see how God has blessed the psalmist.

119.88 be good to me; some Hebrew manuscripts have save me from death.

119.96 has limits...is perfect; or comes to an end...is permanent.

119.109 I am always ready to risk my life; I; or My life is in constant danger, but I.

119.119 You treat all the wicked like; one ancient Hebrew manuscript has I regard all the wicked as.

119.128 Some ancient translations all your instructions; Hebrew unclear.

119.160 truth; or permanence.

(121)

Psalm 120   A prayer for help by one who is persecuted by enemies.

120.5   Meshech...Kedar: two distant regions, whose people were regarded as savages.

Psalm 121   A hymn expressing confidence in God's protection.

121.1   The mountains: either where the Temple stood, or the places where pagan gods were worshiped.

Psalm 122   A song in praise of Jerusalem, where God dwells with his people.

122.1   The LORD's house: the Temple in Jerusalem.

Psalm 123   A prayer for God's protection from hostile opponents.

Psalm 124   A hymn of thanksgiving to God for protecting his people.

124.4   Flood...water...torrent: figures of dangers (see 69.1).

Psalm 125   In praise of God's protection and care.

125.1   Mount Zion: see 2.6.

125.5   The wicked: pagans.
Those who abandon your ways: faithless Israelites.

Psalm 126   A prayer in which the returned exiles pray to be saved from dangers and difficulties.

126.1   brought us back to Jerusalem; or made Jerusalem prosperous again.

126.4   make us prosperous again; or take us back to our land.

Psalm 127   A meditation on God's goodness to his faithful people.

127.1   house: either a person's home or God's home, the Temple.

Psalm 128   A meditation on the blessings that God bestows on his faithful people.

128.5   Zion: either the Temple or the city of Jerusalem.

Psalm 129   A prayer asking God to punish Israel's enemies.

129.1   Young: when Israel came into being as a nation at the exodus from Egypt.

129.5   Zion: either Jerusalem or the land of Israel.

129.6   Housetops: on the flat clay roofs of Palestinian homes weeds and grass would grow wild.

Psalm 130   A prayer for forgiveness and help by one who is in despair.

Psalm 131   A humble prayer of confidence in God's guidance.

Psalm 132   In praise of Jerusalem, the Temple, King David, and his royal descendants.

132.5   See Acts 7.46.

132.6   Covenant Box: a small wooden chest in which were kept, among other things, the two stone tablets on which were inscribed the Ten Commandments (see Exo 25.10-22).
Jearim: the town of Kiriath Jearim, some 15 kilometers northwest of Jerusalem; the place to which the Covenant Box was returned after having been captured in battle by the Philistines (see 1 Sam 6.13--7.2).

132.7   The LORD's house: the Temple in Jerusalem.
His throne: the Covenant Box, in the Most Holy Place of the Temple.

132.13   Zion: either the Temple or the city of Jerusalem.

Psalm 133   A meditation on the happiness of fellowship and harmony.

133.2   Mount Hermon: see 29.6.

Psalm 134   A call for the priests to praise God.

134.3   Zion: either the Temple or the city of Jerusalem.

Psalm 135   A hymn in praise of the LORD, the one true God.

135.3   he is kind; or it is pleasant to do so.

135.7   His storeroom: see similar description in 33.7.

135.11   See Num 21.21-35; Deut 2.30-33; 3.1-6.
Amorites: one of the names used of the original inhabitants of Canaan.
Bashan: a region northeast of Lake Galilee.

135.18   May all...become; or All who made them and trust in them will become.

135.20   Levites: members of the tribe of Levi who assisted the priests in the Temple services.

Psalm 136   In praise of God as creator of the universe and savior of his people.

136.6   The deep waters: see 24.2.

136.13 Red Sea: see 106.7.

136.19-20 See 135.11

Psalm 137   A lament and a cry for vengeance by Israelites in exile
in Babylonia.

137.1   Zion: Jerusalem, or the Temple.

137.7   The Edomites: people of Edom, a country south of the Dead Sea,
who helped the Babylonians when they destroyed Jerusalem in
587 B.C. (see Ezek 35.5; Obadiah 10-14).

137.8   you will be destroyed; or you destroyer.

Psalm 138   A prayer of thanksgiving to God for his power and love.

138.1   The gods: God in heaven was surrounded by the gods of the other
nations (see 82.1).

138.2   Probable text your name and your commands are supreme; Hebrew
your command is greater than all your name.

Psalm 139   A prayer of trust by one who is certain that the all-knowing
God will protect him in all circumstances.

139.15 my mother's womb; or the depths of the earth.

139.16 Your book: see 56.8.

139.17 how difficult I find your thoughts; or how precious are your
thoughts to me.

139.18 When I awake; some Hebrew manuscripts have When I finish count-
ing them.

139.20 Probable text they speak...name; Hebrew unclear.

139.24 the everlasting way; or the way of my ancestors.

Psalm 140   A prayer for protection by one whose life is threatened by
enemies.

140.3   Their tongues...their words: either false accusations or
magical curses.

140.9   Probable text Don't let my enemies be victorious; Hebrew unclear.

140.10 A pit: Sheol, the world of the dead (see 6.5).

Psalm 141   A prayer for protection from enemies and for deliverance
from temptation.

141.2   Incense: a powder ground from aromatic spices which was used with
        sacrifices.
        Uplifted hands: the attitude of prayer.

141.7   Verses 5-7 in Hebrew are unclear.

141.10 See 7.15-16.

Psalm 142   A prayer for help by one who is persecuted by enemies.

        Hebrew title: see 1 Sam 22.1-2.

142.3   he knows what I should do; or he takes care of me.

142.5   want; or need.

142.7   distress; or prison.
        Assembly: see 26.12.

Psalm 143   A prayer for help by one who trusts in God's righteousness
        and love.

Psalm 144   A king's prayer of thanksgiving to God for having given
        him victory over his enemies.

144.7   Deep water: a figure of distress and danger.

Psalm 145   In praise to God for his love and care.

Psalm 146   A call to praise God and to trust in him alone.

146.4   The dust: see 104.29.

146.10 Zion: either Jerusalem or the land of Israel.

Psalm 147   In praise of God, the creator of the universe and savior
        of his people.

147.2   The exiles: from the Babylonian captivity.

147.6   ground; or world of the dead.

147.7   Harp: see 33.2.

Psalm 148   A call for all creation to praise God.

148.4   Waters above the sky: a reference to the waters above the
        celestial dome (see Gen 1.6-7).

148.6   by his command...disobey; or he has fixed them in their places
        for all time, by a command that lasts forever.

(125)

<u>Psalm 149</u>   A hymn of praise to God for protecting his people.

149.1   <u>Assembly</u>: see 26.12.

149.2   <u>Zion</u>: either Jerusalem or the land of Israel.

<u>Psalm 150</u>   A call to praise God; the concluding doxology of Book Five (Psalms 107-150) and of the whole psalter.

150.3   <u>Harps and lyres</u>: see 33.2.

PROVERBS

1.1   <u>Solomon</u>: it is reported that he composed 3,000 proverbs (1 <u>Kgs 4.32</u>).

1.7   To have knowledge...LORD; <u>or</u> The most important part of knowledge is having reverence for the LORD.

1.8   <u>Son</u>: not implying the speaker is his father but rather his teacher.

1.19   <u>One ancient translation</u> what happens to; <u>Hebrew</u> the path of.

1.21   <u>City gates</u>: near which people gathered for social, commercial, and judicial purposes.

2.1   <u>Son</u>: see 1.8.

2.18   <u>World of the dead</u>: thought of as a dark abyss in the depths of the earth.

3.1   <u>Son</u>: see 1.8.

3.12   <u>Verses 11-12 are quoted in Hebrews 12.5-6 as they appear in the ancient Greek translation, the Septuagint.</u>

3.34   <u>This verse is quoted in James 4.6 and 1 Peter 5.5 as it appears in the ancient Greek translation, the Septuagint.</u>

4.8   Embrace her; <u>or</u> Prize her highly.

4.10   <u>Son</u>: see 1.8.

5.6   <u>Some ancient translations</u> She does not stay; <u>Hebrew</u> Or else she will stay.

5.14   And suddenly I found myself; <u>or</u> I was about to be.

6.30   People don't despise...hungry; <u>or</u> Don't people despise...hungry?

(126)

7.14   The meat from the sacrifices: only part of the animal offered
in certain sacrifices was burned on the altar; the rest of the
meat was kept by the worshiper.

7.22   Probable text like a deer prancing into a trap; Hebrew unclear.

8.3   The gates: see 1.21.

8.27   The sky: thought of as a solid dome (see Gen 1.6-8; Job 37.18).

8.29   Earth's foundations: it was thought that the surface of the
earth was supported by pillars which rested on a solid foundation
beneath the seas.

8.31   an architect; or a little child.

9.13   Verse 13 in Hebrew is unclear.

9.17   This popular saying apparently refers to adultery.

10.10   One ancient translation but one who openly criticizes works for
peace; Hebrew repeats verse 8b.

10.22   Hard work can make you no richer; or And the LORD does not add
sorrow to your wealth.

11.4   Save your life: that is, keep you from premature death (also
10.2).

11.16   One ancient translation but a woman...money; Hebrew does not
have these words.

11.19   Will die: that is, before his time (see 11.4).

11.23   everyone is angry; or God punishes them.

11.30   One ancient translation Righteousness; Hebrew A righteous man.
Probable text violence; Hebrew a wise man.

11.31   This verse is quoted in 1 Peter 4.18 as it appears in the ancient
Greek translation, the Septuagint.

12.12   Verse 12 in Hebrew is unclear.

12.27   Verse 27 in Hebrew is unclear.

12.28   One ancient translation wickedness; Hebrew path.

13.15   One ancient translation road to ruin; Hebrew permanent road.

13.23   Verse 23 in Hebrew is unclear.

14.4   your barn will be...grain; or you may grow a little grain, but with them you can grow much more.

14.9   Verse 9 in Hebrew is unclear.

14.14   Probable text for their deeds; Hebrew from upon them.

14.17   One ancient translation remain calm; Hebrew are hated.

14.24   Probable text are known by; Hebrew unclear.

14.27   Death: see 11.19.

14.32   Some ancient translations integrity; Hebrew death.

14.33   One ancient translation nothing; Hebrew does not have this word.

15.11   World of the dead: see 2.18.

16.1   has the last word; or inspires our words.

16.7   you can make; or he will make.

16.12   Kings cannot tolerate evil; or It is intolerable for kings to do evil.

16.33   Cast lots: specially marked stones were used to determine God's will; it is not known precisely how they were used (see also Deut 33.8).

17.18   With no sense: a warning against rashly offering to pay someone's debts, especially those of a stranger (see 6.1-5; 20.16).

17.19   brag all the time; or make a show of your wealth.

18.18   Casting lots: see 16.33.

18.19   Some ancient translations Help...wall; Hebrew unclear.

18.24   Some ancient translations Some friendships do; Hebrew a man of friends does.

19.7   Probable text No matter...any; Hebrew unclear.

19.18   If you...themselves; or But don't punish them so hard that you kill them.

19.19   get him out...again; or try to get him out of trouble, you only make things worse.

19.22   It is a disgrace to be greedy; or Loyalty is what is desired in a person.

(128)

20.16   Stupid enough: see 17.18.

22.26   Someone else's debts: see 17.18.

22.28   Property line: marked by stones, which were easily moved.

23.1   keep in mind who he is; or notice carefully what is before you.

23.10   Property line: see 22.28.

23.26   Son: see 1.8.

24.3   Homes are built on the foundation of wisdom and understanding; or It takes care to lay the foundation of a house, and craftsmanship to build it.

24.5   Some ancient translations Being wise is better than being strong; Hebrew A man is wise in strength.

24.21   Son: see 1.8.

25.1   Hezekiah: ruled 716-687 B.C.

25.2   What he conceals: God's ways cannot always be understood, yet we honor him; kings, however, must explain their actions.

25.27   Probable text and so...praise; Hebrew unclear.

26.8   Sling: used for throwing stones (see 1 Sam 17.40,49-50).

26.10   Verse 10 in Hebrew is unclear.

26.23   One ancient translation Insincere; Hebrew Burning. Probable text fine glaze; Hebrew unrefined silver.

27.9   One ancient translation but trouble shatters your peace of mind; Hebrew unclear.

27.11   Son: see 1.8.

27.13   Stupid enough: see 17.18. One ancient translation stranger's debts; Hebrew stranger's debts or those of an immoral woman.

27.16   Probable text or ever...oil?; Hebrew unclear.

29.5   yourself; or them.

29.10   Probable text protect; Hebrew seek.

29.21   he will take over everything you own; or you will not be able to control him.

30.1   Probable text "God...helpless; Hebrew unclear.

30.17   One ancient translation mother in her old age; Hebrew mother's obedience.

30.31   Verse 31 in Hebrew is unclear.

31.6   Dying...in misery: for such people alcoholic drinks serve as a painkiller.

ECCLESIASTES

1.1   Philosopher; or Teacher. The English name of the book, Ecclesiastes, represents the Greek translation of the Hebrew name Qoheleth, which is formed from the word "gathering, assembly."

1.8   Everything; or Words.

2.14   Same fate: death (see 3.19).

3.1   At the time God chooses: that is, all occasions have been set, and human beings are unable to make any changes.

3.17   Probable text its own set time; Hebrew its own set time there.

3.21   spirit...spirit; or breath...breath.

3.22   what we have...do; or our work, because we are going to have to do it anyway.

5.6   priest; or angel.

5.9   Verse 9 in Hebrew is unclear.

5.13   for a time when they may need it; or to their own hurt.

5.17   Some ancient translations in darkness and grief; Hebrew eating in darkness.

6.6   Same place: Sheol, the world of the dead.

6.10   and we all know that a man; or and a man's nature is already known; a man.

7.14   you never know what is going to happen next; or you cannot find fault with him.

8.2   Some ancient translations Do what the king says; Hebrew unclear.

8.10   Verse 10 in Hebrew is unclear.

9.2　　hate. No one...difference; or hate, but no one knows whether it
is out of love or hate. [2]It makes no difference what lies ahead
of us.
　　　　Some ancient translations and the bad; Hebrew does not have
these words.

9.10　　World of the dead: thought of as a vast abyss in the depths of
the earth.

9.15　　he could have...him; or he saved the town.　But later on no one
remembered him.

10.4　　keep calm; or submit to him.

12.1　　The Hebrew phrase for your Creator sounds like the Hebrew for
your grave.

12.12　Son: see Prov 1.8.

SONG OF SONGS

1.1　　by Solomon; or dedicated to Solomon, or about Solomon.

1.5　　but; or and.
　　　　Kedar: a region in northern Arabia.

1.7　　Probable text Why should I...shepherds; Hebrew unclear.

1.9　　Pharaoh: the title of the king of Egypt.

1.13　Myrrh: an aromatic substance, made from the hardened sap of
a tree.

1.14　Engedi: an oasis on the west bank of the Dead Sea.

2.1　　Sharon: a coastal plain in the northern part of Palestine.

2.5　　Apples: thought to stimulate sexual vigor.

2.11　Winter: the rainy season.

2.15　Foxes...our vineyard: apparently a figure of violent men who
threaten to violate the girl.

2.17　Mountains of Bether; or rugged mountains.

3.6　　Myrrh: see 1.13.

4.1　　Gilead: on the east side of the Jordan River.

4.4　　Probable text round and smooth; Hebrew unclear.

4.8   Mount Amana...Mount Senir...Mount Hermon: in the mountain ranges east of Lebanon.

5.12   Probable text and standing by the stream; Hebrew unclear.

5.14   Probable text like smooth ivory; Hebrew unclear.

6.4   Tirzah: at one time the capital of the northern kingdom of Israel (see 1 Kgs 14.17).
Probable text as breathtaking as these great cities; Hebrew unclear.

6.8   Concubines: women of the royal harem.

6.10   Probable text as dazzling as the sun or the moon; Hebrew unclear.

6.12   Verse 12 in Hebrew is unclear.

6.13   Dance, dance; or Come back, come back.
Shulam: if a place name, its location is unknown.

7.4   Heshbon: in Moab, on the east side of the Dead Sea.

7.5   Mount Carmel: in the northern part of the country, near the Mediterranean.
Probable text beauty; Hebrew unclear.

7.9   Some ancient translations lips and teeth; Hebrew lips of those who sleep.

7.11   villages; or fields.

7.13   Mandrakes: plants used as love charms (see Gen 30.14).

8.11   Baal Hamon: location unknown.

ISAIAH

1.1   Uzziah, Jotham, Ahaz, and Hezekiah: kings of Judah from 781 to 687 B.C.; Uzziah was king 781-740 and Hezekiah 716-687.

1.2   The children I brought up: the people of Israel.

1.7   Devastated: a reference either to the invasion by the Assyrian emperor Tiglath-Pileser III in 734-733 B.C. or to the invasion by the Assyrian emperor Sennacherib in 701 B.C. (see 36.1).

1.9   Sodom and Gomorrah: see Gen 19.24-25.

1.18   sin, but I will wash you as clean as snow; or sin; do you think
I will wash you as clean as snow?
     Although your...wool; or Your stains are deep red; do you think
you will be as white as wool?

1.29   Sacred gardens: it was believed that dedicating a garden to a
fertility god would cause him to bless the crops.

2.3   Hill of the LORD: Mount Zion, the hill in Jerusalem which
formed part of the Temple and palace area.

2.6   Probable text; The land...Philistia; Hebrew unclear.
Philistia: a federation of five cities along the southern
Mediterranean coast, west of Judah.

2.13   Bashan: a region northeast of Lake Galilee.

3.9   Sodom: see Gen 19.1-11.

3.10   Probable text Righteous men will be happy; Hebrew Say to the
righteous.

3.13   Some ancient translations his people; Hebrew the peoples.

3.14   Elders: probably men who settled disputes.

4.5   Cloud...smoke and a bright flame: means by which God led his
people through the wilderness (see Exo 13.21).

5.2   Tower: from the top of which a watchman would keep watch over
the vineyard.

5.3   My vineyard: Israel, the people of God (see verse 7).

5.14   World of the dead: thought of as a vast abyss in the depths of
the earth.

5.17   Verse 17 in Hebrew is unclear.

5.26   Probable text a distant nation; Hebrew distant nations.
A distant nation: probably Assyria.

6.1   The year that King Uzziah died: 740 B.C.
His throne: the Covenant Box in the Most Holy Place in the
Temple (see Exo 25.21-22).

6.2   Flaming creatures: in Hebrew Seraphim, "fiery ones," heavenly
beings serving as God's attendants.
     Body: euphemism for private parts.

6.10   Verses 9-10 are quoted in Matt 13.14-15 and Acts 28.26-27 as
they appear in the ancient Greek translation, the Septuagint.

7.1   Ahaz: king of Judah 736-716 B.C.

7.3   Shear Jashub: this name in Hebrew means "A few will come back"
(see 10.20-22).
Upper pool: the reservoir south of the Pool of Siloam, at the
southeast corner of Jerusalem.

7.6   Tabeel's son: his name is not given, and nothing is known about
Tabeel himself.

7.11   World of the dead: see 5.14.

7.13   Descendants of King David: the kings of Judah.

7.14   Young woman: the Hebrew word here translated "young woman" is
not the specific term for "virgin," but refers to any young
woman of marriageable age. The use of "virgin" in Matt 1.23
reflects the ancient Greek translation of the Old Testament, the
Septuagint, made some 500 years after Isaiah.
Immanuel: this name in Hebrew means "God is with us."

7.15   Milk and...honey: simple foods which suggest difficult times
(see verse 22).

7.17   Israel separated from Judah: after the death of King Solomon
in 931 B.C.

7.20   He will shave off: a figure of complete defeat and humiliation.

8.1   large letters: or letters that everyone could read.

8.2   The priest Uriah: see 2 Kgs 16.10-16.

8.6   Shiloah Brook: a stream which flowed from the large spring on
the eastern side of Jerusalem.
tremble; Hebrew rejoice.

8.8   everything." God...land; or everything. They will spread out
over the land. God be with us!"

8.18   Mount Zion: see 2.3.

8.20   Verse 20 in Hebrew is unclear.

9.1   Zebulun and Naphtali: in the northern part of the country,
west of Lake Galilee.

9.3   Probable text You have given them great joy; Hebrew You have
increased the nation.

9.4   Defeated the army of Midian: see Judges 7.1-25; Midian was on
the east side of the Gulf of Aqaba.

9.6   Wonderful; or Wise.

9.9   Samaria: the capital of the northern kingdom of Israel.

9.10   Brick...sycamore: ordinary building material; stone...cedar:
expensive building material.

9.11   Probable text their enemies; Hebrew the enemies of Rezin.

9.21   Manasseh and...Ephraim: two tribes of the northern kingdom of
Israel; Judah: the southern kingdom.

10.1   You; the rulers of Israel.

10.9   Calno...Carchemish...Hamath and Arpad: cities in northern Syria;
Damascus: the capital of Syria.

10.23 Verses 22-23 are quoted in Rom 9.27-28 as they appear in the
ancient Greek translation, the Septuagint.

10.24 Zion: Jerusalem.

10.26 Oreb Rock: see Judges 7.23-25.

10.27 Hebrew has three additional words, the meaning of which is
unclear.

10.28 Ai: this and the other places mentioned in verses 28-32 were
located near Jerusalem, along the way by which an invader would
come to attack from the north.

11.9   God's holy hill: see 2.3.

11.10 This verse is quoted in Rom 15.12 as it appears in the ancient
Greek translation, the Septuagint.

11.11 Pathros: southern Egypt; Elam: southeast of Mesopotamia, in
what is now Iran; Hamath: a city in Syria.

11.14 Edom: south of the Dead Sea; Moab: on the east side of the
Dead Sea; Ammon: on the east side of the Jordan River.

13.17 Medes: people of Media, a nation northeast of Babylonia which
became part of the Persian Empire.

13.19 Sodom and Gomorrah: see 1.9.

13.22 Probable text towers; Hebrew widows.

14.8   Cuts them down: to use for building palaces.

14.9   World of the dead: see 5.14.

(135)

14.12　Bright morning star: a title of divinity, a figurative way of speaking of the Babylonian king's past power and fame.

14.13　That mountain: known as Mount Zaphon, north of Ugarit, where according to popular belief the gods assembled.

14.28　The year that King Ahaz died: 716 B.C.; he was succeeded by Hezekiah.

14.29　The rod: probably an Assyrian emperor, perhaps Sargon II, who died 705 B.C.

14.31　Philistine cities: Ashkelon, Ashdod, Ekron, Gaza, and Gath, all of them on or near the Mediterranean coast.

14.32　Zion: either Jerusalem or the whole kingdom of Judah.

15.1　Moab: see 11.14.

15.2　Probable text people of Dihon; Hebrew people and Dihon.

15.3　Sackcloth: garments made of coarse material, worn as a sign of mourning.

16.2　Arnon River: Moab's largest river, flowing west into the Dead Sea.

16.7　Kir Heres: the same as Kir in 15.1.

16.10　One ancient translation the shouts of joy are ended; Hebrew I have ended the shouts of joy.

16.12　To pray: to their god Chemosh (see Num 21.29).

17.1　Damascus: the capital of Syria.

17.2　One ancient translation The cities of Syria will be deserted forever; Hebrew The cities of Aroer are deserted.

17.5　Rephaim Valley: probably southwest of Jerusalem.

17.8　Asherah: Canaanite goddess of fertility.

17.9　One ancient translation the Hivites and the Amorites; Hebrew woodland and hill country.
Hivites...Amorites: original inhabitants of Canaan (see Deut 7.1).

17.10　Sacred gardens: see 1.29.
A foreign god: Adonis, god of vegetation.

18.1　Wings: of flying insects, especially mosquitoes, which abounded in that region.

18.2   Ambassadors come: to propose that Judah form an alliance with Egypt against Assyria. The prophet orders them to go back home.

19.4   Tyrant: probably the emperor of Assyria; it could be an oppressive Egyptian king.

19.11   Zoan: on the delta of the Nile, and at one time the capital of Egypt.

19.13   Memphis: at one time the capital of Egypt.

19.18   Five: meaning here a few.

19.23   the two nations will worship together; or the Egyptians will be slaves to the Assyrians.

20.1   Sargon II: emperor of Assyria 727-705 B.C.
        Attacked: in 711 B.C.

20.2   Sackcloth: see 15.3.

20.3   Ashdod: see 14.31.

21.2   Elam: see 11.11; Media: see 13.17. These two countries joined the Persians in attacking and conquering Babylon in 539 B.C.

21.11   Edom: see 11.14.

21.13   Dedan: a city in northern Arabia.

21.14   Tema: a city in northwest Arabia.

21.16   Kedar: in northern Arabia.

22.1   Valley of Vision: perhaps a reference to Hinnom Valley, south of Jerusalem.

22.6   Elam: see 11.11.
        Kir: location uncertain.

22.8   The arsenal: probably the Hall of the Forest of Lebanon, built by Solomon (see 1 Kgs 7.2; 10.17).

22.12   Shave your heads and wear sackcloth: as signs of mourning (see 15.3).

22.15   Manager of the royal household: during the reign of King Hezekiah (see 36.3).

22.20   Eliakim son of Hilkiah: see 36.1--37.6.

22.22   The king: Hezekiah (see verse 15).

(137)

23.1   Tyre: a Phoenician city on the Mediterranean coast, north of
        Palestine.

23.2   Sidon: a Phoenician city on the Mediterranean coast, north of
        Tyre.

23.10   Verse 10 in Hebrew is unclear.

23.13   Verse 13 in Hebrew is unclear.

24.1   Devastate the earth: chapters 24--27 contain a series of
        messages about the final judgment of the LORD and the destruction
        of the earth.

24.5   The covenant: perhaps a reference to God's covenant with Noah
        (Gen 9.8-17).

24.21   Powers above: gods who were believed to control the stars.

25.4   Probable text winter storm; Hebrew storm against a wall.

25.10   Mount Zion: see 14.32.
        Moab: see 11.14. The mention of Moab here is unexpected, and
        perhaps is to be understood as representing all of Israel's
        enemies.

26.12   everything that...do; or you treat us according to what we do.

26.16   Verse 16 in Hebrew is unclear.

26.18   Probable text We have won...nothing; Hebrew unclear.

27.1   Leviathan...monster: legendary monsters which were symbols of
        the nations oppressing Israel. In this passage Leviathan may
        represent Assyria and Babylonia, and the sea monster, Egypt.

27.2   His pleasant vineyard: his people Israel (see 5.1-7).

27.9   Asherah: see 17.8.

27.10   The fortified city: of Israel's enemy.

27.13   Sacred hill: see 2.3.

28.2   Someone: the emperor of Assyria.

28.11   Foreigners: the Assyrians.

28.15   World of the dead: see 5.14; perhaps here a symbol for Egypt.

28.16   This verse is quoted in 1 Peter 2.6 as it appears in the ancient
        Greek translation, the Septuagint.

28.17 Plumb line: a line with a weight attached which was used to determine whether a wall was completely straight; used here as a figure.

28.21 Mount Perazim: probably near Rephaim Valley (see 2 Sam 5.17-20). Gibeon: a city about 10 kilometers northwest of Jerusalem (see Josh 10.10-12).

28.25 Hebrew has an additional word, the meaning of which is unclear.

29.1 Jerusalem: in Hebrew Ariel, a word which may mean "lion of God" or "mountain of God" or "city of God" or "altar of God."

29.13 This verse is quoted in Matt 15.8-9 and Mark 7.6-7 as it appears in the ancient Greek translation, the Septuagint.

29.14 The second half of this verse is quoted in 1 Cor 1.19 as it appears in the ancient Greek translation, the Septuagint.

30.2 They go to Egypt: around 703 B.C. the kingdom of Judah tried to make an alliance with Egypt against Assyria.

30.33 the emperor of Assyria; or for Molech (see 2 Kgs 23.10).

31.1 Go to Egypt: see 30.2.

32.19 Verse 19 seems to be a later addition to the text.

33.1 Our enemies: perhaps the Babylonians.

33.9 Sharon: the fertile plain extending along the Mediterranean coast, between Mount Carmel (to the north) and Joppa (to the south). Bashan: the region northeast of Lake Galilee.

33.11 One ancient translation My spirit is like a fire that will destroy you; Hebrew You are destroying yourselves.

33.21 Verse 21 in Hebrew is unclear.

34.5 Edom: see 11.14.

34.6 Bozrah: a city in northern Edom.

34.8 Zion: either Jerusalem or the whole kingdom of Judah.

34.12 Verse 12 in Hebrew begins with a word, the meaning of which is unclear.

34.14 Night monster: a female demon, believed to live in desolate places.

34.17 The land: Edom.

35.2   Carmel and Sharon: see 33.9.

35.8   Probable text no fools...follow it; Hebrew unclear.

36.1   Fourteenth year: 701 B.C.

36.2   Lachish: some 35 kilometers southwest of Jerusalem.
       Upper pool: see 7.3.

36.11 Aramaic: the language of Syria (Aram), which had become the
       common language of the various peoples of that part of the world.

36.19 Hamath and Arpad: see 10.9.
       Sepharvaim: a city whose location is uncertain.
       Samaria: the capital of the northern kingdom of Israel, which
       was now ruled by the Assyrians.

37.8   Lachish: see 36.2.

37.16 Winged creatures: figures which symbolized God's majesty and
       were associated with his presence with his people; see a descrip-
       tion of them in Exo 25.18-20.

37.27 Probable text when the hot east wind blasts them; Hebrew blasted
       before they are grown.

37.38 Ararat: in what later became Armenia (now a part of Turkey).

38.22 Verses 21-22 are moved here from the end of the chapter (see
       2 Kgs 20.6-9).

38.8   stairway...ten steps ...ten steps; or sundial...ten degrees...
       ten degrees (see 2 Kgs 20.11).

38.10 World of the dead: see 5.14.

38.11 See the LORD: take part in the worship in the Temple.

38.12 Probable text I thought that God was ending my life; Hebrew
       unclear.

38.13 Verse 13 in Hebrew is unclear.

38.15 One ancient translation I cannot sleep; Hebrew unclear.

38.16 One ancient translation I will live for you, for you alone;
       Hebrew unclear.

38.17 Some ancient translations save; Hebrew love.

38.18   Can praise you: it was believed that in Sheol, the world of
         the dead (see 5.14), it was impossible to have communion with God.

38.20   Verses 21-22 are placed after verse 6.

39.7   Made eunuchs: castrated.

40.2   Suffered: the exile in Babylonia.
         and their sins are now forgiven; or they have paid for what
         they did.

40.3   This verse is quoted in Matt 3.3; Mark 1.3; Luke 3.4; and
         John 1.23 as it appears in the ancient Greek translation, the
         Septuagint.

40.5   The glory of the LORD: his saving presence with his people.

40.9   Jerusalem, go up...news!; or Go up on a high mountain and pro-
         claim the good news to Jerusalem! Call out with a loud voice and
         announce the good news to Zion!

40.10   the people he has rescued; or the rewards he has for his people.
         Rescued: from exile in Babylonia.

40.20   Verses 19-20a in Hebrew are unclear.

41.2   The conquerer from the east: Cyrus, emperor of Persia 555-529
         B.C., who conquered Babylonia in 539 B.C. and in the following
         year allowed the Jews to return home from exile in Babylonia (see
         Ezra 1.1-4).

41.15   Threshing board: an implement used to thresh grain, with sharp
         pieces of iron or stone fastened underneath it.
         You will thresh: a figure describing how Israel will defeat
         other countries.

41.25   A man who lives in the east: see 41.2.

41.27   Verse 27 in Hebrew is unclear.

42.1   My servant: verses 1-4 comprise the first of four poems about
         the LORD's Servant (also 49.1-6; 50.4-11; 52.13--53.12); some
         interpret the Servant to be the nation of Israel, others to be an
         individual.

42.3   A bent reed...a flickering lamp: figures of people who are
         helpless and weak.

42.4   The last part of verse 4 is quoted in Matt 12.21 as it appears
         in the ancient Greek translation, the Septuagint.

42.5   <u>Stretched them out</u>: like a curtain or the flaps of a tent (see 40.22).

42.11   <u>Kedar</u>: see 21.16; <u>Sela</u>: a city in Edom; these two places represent all distant countries.

42.15   <u>Probable text</u> deserts; <u>Hebrew</u> coastlands.

42.24   <u>The looters</u>: the Assyrian and the Babylonian invaders.

43.3   <u>Seba</u>: probably a region in Africa, south of Egypt.

43.16   <u>The sea</u>: a reference to the escape from Egypt and the destruction of the Egyptian forces (see Exo 14.1-31).

43.19   <u>The new thing</u>: the return of the Jews from exile to their homeland.

43.27   <u>Your earliest ancestor</u>: Jacob; perhaps Abraham (see 51.2).

43.28   <u>One ancient translation</u> your rulers profaned; <u>Hebrew</u> I profaned the rulers of.

44.5   <u>Mark...on his arm</u>: perhaps the initial letter Y of the LORD's name (Yahweh).

44.7   Verse 7 in Hebrew is unclear.

44.20   It makes as much sense; <u>or</u> It will do him as much good.

44.28   <u>Cyrus</u>: see 41.2.

45.1   <u>Chosen</u>: in Hebrew <u>mashiah</u>, from which English "messiah" comes; in <u>Greek christos</u>, from which "Christ" comes. <u>Cyrus</u>: see 41.2.

45.14   <u>Seba</u>: see 43.3.

45.20   <u>The empire</u>: the Babylonian empire, conquered by Cyrus in 539 B.C.

46.11   <u>A man...from the east</u>: see 41.2.

47.2   <u>Turn the millstone</u>: the work of a slave. <u>Cross the streams</u>: probably a reference to going into exile.

47.13   <u>Some ancient translations</u> what; <u>Hebrew</u> from what.

48.2   <u>The holy city</u>: Jerusalem.

48.6   <u>New things</u>: see 43.19.

48.10   <u>The fire of suffering</u>: the exile in Babylonia.

48.13   Earth's foundations: it was believed that the surface of the
earth was supported by pillars which rested on a foundation in
the depths of the seas.

48.14   The man I have chosen: Cyrus (see 41.2).

48.16   And sent me: the speaker of this parenthetical statement is
unknown; perhaps it is Cyrus.

48.21   Water...from a rock: see Exo 17.1-7.

49.1   His servant: verses 1-6 comprise the second poem about the LORD's
Servant (see 42.1). In verse 3 he is the nation Israel, and in
verse 5 he is someone other than the people of Israel.

49.2   With his own hand he protected me; or He kept me hidden in his
hand.

49.12   Aswan: a city in southern Egypt, where a large Jewish community
had settled.

50.4   Me: the servant of the LORD; verses 4-11 comprise the third
poem about the LORD's Servant (see 42.1).

51.9   Rahab: a legendary sea monster, which represented the forces of
chaos and evil, was sometimes a symbol of Egypt.

51.13   Earth's foundations: see 48.13.

51.16   One ancient translation stretched out; Hebrew planted.

52.8   Those who guard the city: the watchmen on the walls, who look
for the return of the exiles to Jerusalem.

52.11   You that carry the Temple equipment: priests and levites; when
the Babylonians captured Jerusalem they took with them utensils
and objects from the Temple (see 2 Kgs 25.13-15; Ezra 1.7-11).
Forbidden thing: any object that was considered ritually unclean.

52.13   My servant: the fourth poem about the LORD's Servant (52.13--
53.12).
he will be highly honored; or he will be restored to greatness
and honor.

52.15   This verse is quoted in Rom 15.21 as it appears in the ancient
Greek translation, the Septuagint.

53.1   what we now report; or what we have heard.

53.8   Verses 7-8 are quoted in Acts 8.32-33 as they appear in the
ancient Greek translation, the Septuagint.

53.12   prayed that they might be forgiven; <u>or</u> suffered the punishment
they deserved.

54.4   <u>Unfaithfulness</u>: Israel's refusal to obey God.
<u>Loneliness</u>: the exile in Babylonia.

54.10   <u>Peace</u>: spiritual and material prosperity and security.

56.7   <u>Sacred hill</u>: see 2.3.

57.9   <u>Molech</u>: the god of the Ammonites, to whom human sacrifices were
sometimes offered (see Lev 18.21).
    <u>World of the dead</u>: some pagan peoples believed it was ruled by
a god.

57.16   I gave my people...forever; <u>or</u> I will not continue to accuse
them or be angry with them forever, for then they would die--the
very people to whom I gave life.

58.3   <u>Fast</u>: a religious duty indicating deep devotion to God's laws.

58.5   <u>Sackcloth and ashes</u>: used to indicate repentance and grief.

60.6   <u>Midian and Ephah...Sheba</u>: places in Arabia.

60.7   <u>Kedar</u>: see 21.16; <u>Nebaioth</u>: in Arabia.

61.1   <u>Verse 1 is quoted in Luke 4.18 as it appears in the ancient
Greek translation, the Septuagint.</u>
    <u>Chosen</u>: see 45.1.

62.6   <u>Sentries</u>: a figure of prophets, who must continually pray that
God will keep his promise.

63.1   <u>Some ancient translations</u> marching along; <u>Hebrew</u> bowed down.

63.10   <u>His holy spirit</u>: the inmost feelings of God, the Holy One;
the phrase is not used in the New Testament sense.

63.11   <u>Probable text</u> they remembered; <u>Hebrew</u> he remembered.

63.18   <u>Verse 18 in Hebrew is unclear.</u>

64.5   <u>Probable text</u> in spite of...ancient times; <u>Hebrew unclear</u>.

64.7   <u>Some ancient translations</u> abandoned; <u>Hebrew</u> melted.

64.10   <u>Your sacred cities</u>: all cities in the land are sacred because
the land itself belongs to God.

65.3   <u>Sacred gardens</u>: see 1.29.

65.4   <u>Pork</u>: forbidden food for the Israelites (see Deut 14.8).

65.10   Plain of Sharon: see 33.9.
         Trouble Valley: probably southwest of Jericho.

65.11   Sacred hill: see 2.3.

65.25   Sacred hill: see 2.3.

66.9   Zion: Jerusalem.

66.17   Sacred gardens: see 1.29.

66.18   Some ancient translations I know; Hebrew I.
         Some ancient translations I am coming; Hebrew He is coming.

66.19   One ancient translation Libya; Hebrew Pul.
         Lydia: a country in what is now western Turkey.
         Tubal: south of the Black Sea, in what is now eastern Turkey.

66.20   Sacred hill: see 2.3.

JEREMIAH

1.1   Anathoth: about 5 kilometers northeast of Jerusalem.

1.2   Thirteenth year: 627 B.C.

1.3   Jehoiakim: ruled 609-598 B.C.
         Eleventh year: 587 B.C.
         Fifth month: Ab, corresponding to modern mid-July to mid-August.

1.5   The nations: Assyria, Babylonia, Egypt, and Judah.

1.6   Too young: probably less than 30 years of age.

1.11   Almond tree: the first to bloom in the spring.

1.12   Watching: this word in Hebrew sounds like the Hebrew for
         "almond."

1.13   The north: a reference to Babylonia (see 20.4).

2.2   Me: that is, God.

2.8   Where is the LORD?: meaning, where and how is he to be worshiped.
         Baal: a Canaanite god of fertility.

2.10   Kedar: in northern Arabia.

2.16   Memphis and Tahpanhes: cities in Egypt.

(145)

2.23   Baal: see 2.8.
       Sinned in the valley: probably a reference to human sacrifices
       in Hinnom Valley (see 7.31).

2.24   Probable text rushing into the desert; Hebrew a wild donkey
       used to the desert.

2.27   A tree...a rock: idols, objects of worship.

3.1   He cannot take her back again: the Law did not allow a twice-
       divorced woman to remarry her first husband (see Deut 24.1-4).

3.6   Josiah was king: 640-609 B.C.

3.8   I divorced Israel and sent her away: the conquest and exile of
       the northern kingdom of Israel by the Assyrians in 722 B.C.

3.14   Mount Zion: the hill in Jerusalem which formed part of the
       Temple and palace area.

3.16   Covenant Box: the symbol of God's presence with his people; it
       was known as God's throne (see Exo 37.1-9).

3.24   Baal: see 2.8.

4.2   it will be right...name. Then; or and if you swear by my
       name and are truthful, just, and righteous, then.

4.6   Zion: Jerusalem.
       The north: see 1.13.

4.7   A destroyer of nations: the king of Babylonia.

4.15   Dan: on the northern border of the country.
       Hills of Ephraim: in the central part of the country.

4.27   This verse appears to be a later addition to the text.

5.12   He won't really do anything; or We don't want anything to do
       with him.

5.26   Probable text they lie in wait...birds; Hebrew unclear.

6.1   Tekoa: about 16 kilometers south of Jerusalem; Beth Haccherem:
       about 3 kilometers south of Jerusalem.

6.20   Sheba: in Arabia (see 1 Kgs 10.1).

6.22   The north: see 1.13.

7.9   Baal: see 2.8.

7.12   Shiloh: the city in the northern kingdom of Israel where the
        Covenant Box was kept in the time of Eli (see 1 Sam 1.3); the city
        was destroyed, probably by the Philistines.

7.18   Queen of Heaven: a pagan fertility goddess, particularly favored
        by women.

7.21   You are permitted to eat: in the fellowship offerings part of
        the animal was burned on the altar and the rest eaten by the
        worshipers (see Lev 3.1).

7.29   Cut off your hair: a sign of mourning.

7.31   Hinnom Valley: to the south and southwest of Jerusalem.

8.13   Probable text Therefore...land; Hebrew unclear.

8.16   Dan: see 4.15.

8.17   Snakes: a figure of deadly dangers.

8.18   Probable text My sorrow cannot be healed; Hebrew unclear.

8.19   Zion: either Jerusalem or the Temple.

8.22   Gilead: a region east of the Jordan, famous for plants that
        were used for medicinal purposes.

9.4   Deceitful as Jacob: see Gen 27.36.

9.14   Baal: see 2.8.

9.15   Bitter herbs...poison: figures of suffering and distress.

9.19   Zion: Jerusalem.

9.25-26 Hair cut short: the desert people cut their hair short in
        honor of their god, a pagan practice forbidden to the Israelites
        (see Lev 19.27).

10.2   Unusual sights in the sky: comets, eclipses and other meteoro-
        logical phenomena, which were interpreted as signs of divine
        displeasure.

10.8   What can they learn from wooden idols?; or What their idols
        teach is worthless.

10.9   Uphaz: location unknown.

10.11   This verse, which is in Aramaic, is a later addition to the
        text.

10.13   Waters above the sky: see Gen 1.6-8.

10.22   A nation to the north: Babylonia (see 1.13).

11.13   Baal: see 2.8.

11.15   One ancient translation promises; Hebrew many.

11.19   Probable text while it is still healthy; Hebrew with its bread.

11.21   Anathoth: Jeremiah's hometown (see 1.1).

12.4   Some ancient translations what we are doing; Hebrew our latter end.

12.16   Baal: see 2.8.

13.4   The Euphrates River: some 640 kilometers from Judah; perhaps the Hebrew word, normally meaning the Euphrates, refers to some place nearer Judah.

13.18   The king and his mother: Jehoiachin and his mother Nehushta (see 2 Kgs 24.8,12).
        Some ancient translations from their heads; Hebrew unclear.

13.21   Probable text What...over you; Hebrew unclear.

14.18   Prophets...doing; or Prophets and priests have been dragged away to a land they know nothing about.

14.19   Zion: Jerusalem.

14.21   Your glorious throne: either the Temple or the Covenant Box (see 3.16).

15.4   Manasseh did: he turned away from God and worshiped idols (see 2 Kgs 21.1-9).

15.6   you because...anger; or you; I was tired of feeling sorry for you.

15.11   Probable text LORD,...served; Hebrew unclear.

15.12   Iron from the north: Babylonia (see 1.13).

16.15   A northern land: see 1.13.

16.16   Fishermen...hunters: symbols of Israel's enemies, the Babylonians.

17.2   Asherah: Canaanite goddess of fertility; her male counterpart was Baal (see 2.8).

17.3   Probable text because of all the sins you have committed; Hebrew your high places for sins.

17.4   Probable text You will have to give up; Hebrew unclear.

17.13   disappear...dust; or go to the world of the dead.

17.16   Probable text to bring disaster on them; Hebrew from being a shepherd after you.

19.2   Hinnom Valley: see 7.31.

19.5   Baal: see 2.8.

19.11   Even in Topheth: because it had been the site of pagan sacrifices (verses 4-5), it was unfit as a place of burial.

20.16   Those cities: Sodom and Gomorrah (see Gen 19.24-25).

21.1   King Zedekiah: the last king of Judah, ruled 598-587 B.C.

21.13   You, Jerusalem, are sitting; or You are enthroned.

22.6   Gilead: on the east side of the Jordan River.

22.10   Joahaz: succeeded Josiah and ruled for three months in 609 B.C. (see 2 Kgs 23.31-34).

22.18   Jehoiakim: succeeded Joahaz and ruled 609-598 B.C. (see 2 Kgs 23.36--24.6).

22.20   Bashan: a region northeast of Lake Galilee.
Moab: on the east side of the Dead Sea.

22.24   Jehoiachin: succeeded Jehoiakim and ruled for three months in 598 B.C. (see 2 Kgs 24.8-16).

23.4   I will not punish them again; or not one of them will be missing.

23.8   A northern land: Babylonia.

23.13   Baal: see 2.8.

23.15   Bitter plants...poison: figures of suffering and distress.

23.33   Burden: the Hebrew word for message and burden is the same.

23.39   Pick them up: the Hebrew verb for pick up comes from the same root as the Hebrew word for message and burden.

24.1   King Jehoiachin...as a prisoner: in 598 B.C. (see 2 Kgs 24.10-12).

(149)

24.8 <u>Zedekiah</u>: succeeded Jehoiachin and ruled 598-587 B.C.

25.1 <u>Fourth year</u>: 605 B.C.

25.23 <u>Cut their hair short</u>: desert peoples (see 9.25-26).

25.29 <u>My own city</u>: Jerusalem.

25.34 <u>Hebrew has an additional word, the meaning of which is unclear.</u> <u>One ancient translation</u> rams; <u>Hebrew</u> vessels.

25.38 The LORD has abandoned his people; <u>or</u> The LORD's people run away.

26.1 <u>Jehoiakim</u>: ruled 609-598 B.C.

26.6 <u>Shiloh</u>: see 7.12.

26.18 <u>Hezekiah</u>: ruled 716-687 B.C.
<u>Micah</u>: see Micah 3.12.

26.21 <u>Jehoiakim</u>: see 26.1.

27.1 <u>Zedekiah</u>: see 24.8.

27.3 <u>Probable text</u> a message; <u>Hebrew</u> them.

27.7 <u>To fall</u>: Babylonia was conquered by the Persians in 539 B.C.

27.19-20 <u>Took away to Babylonia</u>: in 598 B.C. (see 24.1).

28.1 <u>One ancient translation</u> That same year; <u>Hebrew</u> That same year at the beginning of his reign.
Fifth month of the fourth year: August 594 B.C.

28.13 <u>One ancient translation</u> he; <u>Hebrew</u> you.

28.17 <u>Seventh month</u>: the Jewish month that began with the first new moon occurring after the modern September 4.

29.8 <u>Probable text</u> their; <u>Hebrew</u> your.

29.11 the future you hope for; <u>or</u> a future full of hope.

29.16 <u>This city</u>: Jerusalem.

29.23 done, and he is a witness against them; <u>or</u> done; he saw them do it.

29.26 <u>Some ancient translations</u> officer; <u>Hebrew</u> officers.

30.14 <u>Your lovers</u>: Israel's allies.

30.17   Zion: the whole country or Jerusalem.

30.21-22   From their own nation: no longer will Israel be under foreign domination.

31.3   One ancient translation them; Hebrew me.

31.4   Tambourine: a small drum with pieces of metal in the rim; generally played by women.

31.6   Ephraim: the northern kingdom of Israel, of which Samaria was the capital.

31.7   Some ancient translations The LORD has saved his; Hebrew LORD, save your.

31.15   Ramah: about 8 kilometers north of Jerusalem, the traditional site of Rachel's tomb (see 1 Sam 10.2).
Rachel is crying for her children: a figure of mourning for the people of the northern kingdom of Israel, conquered and taken into exile by the Assyrians in 722 B.C.

31.20   I mention your name, I think; or I threaten to punish, I still think.

31.22   Probable text as different...man; Hebrew unclear.

31.23   Sacred hill: Mount Zion, the hill in Jerusalem which formed part of the Temple and palace area.

31.26   So then...refreshed.'; or Then I woke up and realized that my dream had been a good one.

31.32   The second part of this verse is quoted in Heb 8.9 as it appears in the ancient Greek translation, the Septuagint.

31.37   Foundations of the earth: it was believed that the surface of the earth was supported by pillars which rested on a foundation in the depths of the seas.

31.38   Hananel Tower: this and the other places named in verses 38-40 are the boundaries of Jerusalem.

32.1   Tenth year: 588 B.C., the year before the fall of Jerusalem (see 24.8).

32.11   Open copy: for easy reference to the conditions of the sale.

32.13   Baruch: Jeremiah's secretary (see 36.4).

32.29   Baal: see 2.8.

32.31   This city: Jerusalem.

32.35   Hinnom Valley: see 7.31.
Molech: the god of the Ammonites, to whom human sacrifices were sometimes offered (see Lev 18.21).

33.5   Probable text in verses 4-5 as a result...houses; Hebrew unclear.

34.7   Lachish: some 35 kilometers southwest of Jerusalem; Azekah: 18 kilometers north of Lachish.

34.21   Has stopped its attack: probably due to the approach of the Egyptian army (see 37.5).

35.1   Jehoiakim: see 26.1.

35.6   Jonadab: see 2 Kgs 10.15-17.

36.1   Fourth year: 605 B.C.

36.9   Ninth month of the fifth year: November 604 B.C.

36.30   No descendant: Jehoiakim's son Jehoiachin was king for three months only (see 2 Kgs 24.5,8-9).

37.1   Zedekiah: brother of Jehoiakim, ruled 598-587 B.C.

37.5   Crossed the Egyptian border: advancing toward Jerusalem, to help the Israelites.

39.1   Tenth month of the ninth year: December 589 B.C.

39.2   Fourth month of the eleventh year: June 587 B.C.

39.3   When Jerusalem was captured: these words are moved here from the end of chapter 38.
The names and titles of these men in Hebrew are unclear.

39.6   Riblah: on the Orontes River, in what is now Syria.

40.1   Ramah: see 31.15.

40.5   When I did not answer; or Then, before he left.

40.6   Mizpah: about 12 kilometers north of Jerusalem.

41.1   Seventh month: the Jewish month that began with the first new moon occurring after the modern September 4.

41.5   Shechem, Shiloh, and Samaria: cities in the northern kingdom of Israel.
Shaved...torn...gashed: signs of distress and mourning.

41.9   One ancient translation was the large one; Hebrew by means of
        Gedaliah.
        King Asa: king of Judah 911-870 B.C.

41.10   Ammon: on the east side of the Jordan River.

41.12   Gibeon: about 10 kilometers northwest of Jerusalem.

42.1   One ancient translation (see also 43.2) Azariah; Hebrew Jezaniah.

43.9   Probable text bury them in the mortar of the pavement; Hebrew
        unclear.

43.10   Some ancient translations he; Hebrew I.
        Some ancient translations you; Hebrew I.

44.17   Queen of Heaven: see 7.18.

44.30   King Hophra: ruled 588-569 B.C.

45.1   Fourth year: 605 B.C.

46.2   Fourth year: 605 B.C.

46.9   Lydia: a country in what is now western Turkey.

46.11   Gilead: see 8.22.

46.16   Probable text Your soldiers have stumbled and fallen; Hebrew
        unclear.

46.18   Mount Tabor...Mount Carmel: two of the tallest mountains in
        Palestine.

46.24   The people of the north: the Babylonians.

46.25   Thebes: the most important city in southern Egypt.

47.1   Gaza: one of the five Philistine cities, on or near the
        Mediterranean coast.

47.4   Tyre and Sidon: Phoenician city-states on the Mediterranean
        coast, allies of the Philistines.
        Crete: the place of origin of the Philistines.

47.5   Ashkelon: another Philistine city.

47.7   The coast: of the Mediterranean Sea.

48.1   Moab: a country east of the Dead Sea.
        Nebo: this and the other places listed in verses 1-3 are cities
        in Moab.

48.13   Bethel: elsewhere in the Old Testament, a town.

48.34   Probable text Heshbon...cry out; Hebrew unclear.

48.36   Kir Heres: the capital city of Moab.

48.37   Shaved...cut off their beards...gashes...sackcloth: signs of
         distress and mourning.

48.38   Housetops: flat, where people went for rest and relaxation.

48.45   Heshbon, the city...flames; or the city of Heshbon, but it is
         in flames and the palace of King Sihon is burning.

49.1   Ammon: a country east of the Jordan River.

49.3   Heshbon: on the border with Moab (see 48.45).

49.7   Edom: to the south of the Dead Sea.

49.8   Esau's descendants: the people of Edom.

49.10   they leave a few...they take only what they want. 10But I; or
         they leave nothing...they take everything. 10And so I.

49.13   Bozrah: a city in northern Edom.

49.18   Sodom and Gomorrah: see Gen 19.24-25.

49.23   Damascus: the capital of Syria.
         Hamath and Arpad: independent Syrian cities, north of Damascus.

49.25   Some ancient translations happy; Hebrew my happiness.

49.28   Kedar: in Arabia.

49.32   People who cut their hair short: desert tribes (see 9.25-26).

49.34   Elam: a country east of Babylonia.
         Zedekiah: ruled 598-587 B.C.

50.5   Zion: Jerusalem.

50.15   Hebrew has an additional word, the meaning of which is unclear.

50.17   Emperor of Assyria: conquered the northern kingdom of Israel
         in 722 B.C.
         King Nebuchadnezzar: conquered the southern kingdom of Judah
         in 587 B.C.

50.19   Bashan: to the northeast of Lake Galilee.
         Gilead: on the east side of the Jordan River.

50.21   One ancient translation them; Hebrew after them.

50.39   demons and evil spirits; or wildcats and jackals.

50.40   Sodom and Gomorrah: see Gen 19.24-25.

51.1   destructive wind; or destroying spirit.

51.11   Media: a country northeast of Babylonia, which joined Persia in the attack on Babylon.

51.16   Waters above the sky: see Gen 1.6-8.

51.27   Ararat, Minni, and Ashkenaz: countries to the north of Babylonia, in what was later Armenia.

51.35   Zion: Jerusalem.

51.59   Fourth year: 594 B.C.

51.64   One ancient translation on it; Hebrew on it and they will become tired out.

52.4   Tenth month of the ninth year: January 588 B.C.

52.5   Eleventh year: 587 B.C.

52.6   Fourth month: the Jewish month that began with the first new moon occurring after the modern June 8.

52.9   Riblah: see 39.5.

52.12   Fifth month of the nineteenth year: July 587 B.C.

52.15   Probable text Babylonia; Hebrew Babylonia some of the poorest people.

52.17   Bronze columns...carts...large bronze tank: see 1 Kgs 7.15-39.

52.28   Seventh year: 598 B.C.

52.29   Eighteenth year: 587 B.C.

52.30   Twenty-third year: 582 B.C.

52.31   Twelfth month of the thirty-seventh year: February 560 B.C.

LAMENTATIONS

1.3   are helpless...home; or fled from home, from the misery of slavery.

1.7   The enemy: the Babylonians.

1.12   Look...by; or May this not happen to you that pass by; or Does this mean nothing to you that pass by?

1.21   One ancient translation Listen; Hebrew They listened.
One ancient translation Bring; Hebrew You brought.

2.1   Zion: Jerusalem.
Temple; or Covenant Box.

2.3   The enemy: see 1.7.

2.10   Dust...sackcloth: signs of distress and mourning.

2.18   Probable text O Jerusalem...Lord; Hebrew Their hearts cried out to the Lord, O wall of Jerusalem.

2.22   My children: the people of Jerusalem.

3.37   The will...out; or No one can make anything happen unless the Lord is willing.

3.39   Why should...sin?; or Why should we complain about being punished for sin, as long as we are still alive?

4.3   Ostriches: see Job 39.14-16.

4.6   punished even more; or more wicked than.
Sodom: see Gen 19.24.

4.7   princes; or Nazirites. (Nazirites: men who took vows to dedicate themselves to God, either for a limited time or indefinitely.)

4.11   Zion: Jerusalem.

4.17   A nation: Egypt; the Judeans hoped Egypt would fight with them against the Babylonians.

4.20   The king: Zedekiah, who ruled 598-587 B.C. (see 2 Kgs 25.1-7).

4.21   Edom: to the south of the Dead Sea.
Uz: location unknown.

4.22   Zion: Jerusalem.

5.14   City gate: the place where people met for commercial, social, and judicial purposes.

5.18   Mount Zion: the hill in Jerusalem which formed part of the Temple and palace area.

EZEKIEL

1.1 Fourth month: the Jewish month that began with the first new
moon occurring after the modern June 8.
Thirtieth year: it is not known to what year this refers;
perhaps to the prophet's age or to the thirtieth year after his
call to be a prophet.
Chebar River: an irrigation canal in Babylonia.

1.2 Taken into exile: in 598 B.C.; the fifth year would be 593 B.C.

1.11 Some ancient translations Two wings; Hebrew Their faces, their
wings.

1.13 Some ancient translations Among; Hebrew And the likeness of.

1.15 Some ancient translations them; Hebrew their faces.

1.18 Verse 18 in Hebrew is unclear.

1.26 Sapphire: a precious stone, blue in color.

2.1 Mortal man: a translation of the Hebrew phrase "son of man,"
which appears almost a hundred times in this book; the phrase
emphasizes the prophet's humanity and mortality, and his need
of God's power to direct him.

3.15 Tel Abib: near the city of Nippur, in Babylonia, not far from
the Chebar canal (see 1.1).

3.23 Chebar River: see 1.1.

4.4-5 Probable text I; Hebrew you.

4.9 Mix them all together: the use of different grains for baking
bread indicates a shortage of food.

4.13 Food which the Law forbids: the Law of Moses prohibited the
eating of certain foods as being ritually unclean (see Lev 11).

4.15 Cow dung: commonly used for fuel; it was not considered ritually
unclean, as was human excrement (verse 12; see Deut 23.13-14).

5.1 Mortal man: see 2.1.
Shave off: a sign of humiliation, inflicted upon a defeated
people.

5.16 Probable text You; Hebrew They.

6.9 Some ancient translations disgraced them; Hebrew I am disgraced.

6.14   Riblah: a city in central Syria, considered the northernmost limit of the country of Israel (see 1 Kgs 8.65).

7.1   Mortal man: see 2.1.

7.7   Probable text celebrations...confusion; Hebrew unclear.

7.10   Probable text Pride is at its height; Hebrew unclear.

7.13   Verse 13 in Hebrew is unclear.

7.16   Verse 16 in Hebrew is unclear.

7.18   Sackcloth...shaved: signs of distress and mourning.

7.22   Temple; or city (that is, Jerusalem).

7.23   One ancient translation Everything is in confusion; Hebrew unclear.

8.1   Sixth month of the sixth year: September 592 B.C.

8.3   Idol: perhaps of the fertility goddess Asherah, which had been originally set up by King Manasseh (see 2 Kgs 21.7).

8.4   Chebar River: see 1.1.

8.10   Unclean animals: the Law of Moses prohibited the eating of certain animals as being ritually unclean (see 4.13; Lev 11).

8.14   Tammuz: a vegetation god who was thought to die when vegetation died and to come to life the next year. Women would mourn his ritual death.

8.17   Offensive way: a reference to a pagan rite of putting a branch to the nose.

9.3   Winged creatures: see 1.5-12.

9.4   A mark: the Hebrew letter tau, written like an X.

9.6   The leaders: the men referred to in 8.16.

9.7   work!" So they began to kill the people in the city.; or work! Go on and start killing the people in the city!"

10.1   The dome: see 1.22.
        Living creatures: see 1.5-12.
        Sapphire: see 1.26.

10.15   Chebar River: see 1.1.

10.19   East gate: facing Kidron Valley and the Mount of Olives on the other side.

10.22   Probable text the faces; Hebrew the faces and them.

11.1   East gate: see 10.19.

11.2   Mortal man: see 2.1.

11.3   We will soon be building houses again; or We won't be building houses any time soon.

11.23   The mountain east of it: Mount of Olives.

12.3   Maybe those rebels will notice you; or Maybe they will then realize that they are rebels.

12.12   The prince: apparently an allusion to King Zedekiah, who was made prisoner by the Babylonians, blinded (see verse 13), and then taken into exile to Babylon (see 2 Kgs 25.4-7).

13.18   Magic wristbands...magic scarves: it is not known exactly how they were thought to possess magic power.

13.20   In verse 20 in Hebrew a word occurs twice, the meaning of which is unclear.

14.3   Mortal man: see 2.1.

14.14   Danel; or Daniel.
        Danel: an ancient hero known for his righteous life.

16.3   You were born in the land of Canaan: Jerusalem was a Jebusite city before being conquered by David and becoming an Israelite city (see 2 Sam 5.6-10).
        Amorite...Hittite: the original inhabitants of the land whom the Israelites regarded as immoral and idolatrous.

16.4   Hebrew has an additional word, the meaning of which is unclear.

16.7   Probable text young woman; Hebrew unclear.

16.8   Covered...with my coat: an act signifying betrothal.

16.15   Sleep with everyone: a figure of idolatry.
        Hebrew has two additional words, the meaning of which is unclear.

16.16   Hebrew has four additional words, the meaning of which is unclear.

16.17   Committed adultery: a figure of idolatry.

16.30   Verse 30 in Hebrew begins with three words, the meaning of which
is unclear.

16.45   Your mother: the original inhabitants of the land, the Canaanites
(see 16.3).

17.2   parable; or allegory.

17.3   Giant eagle: the Babylonian king Nebuchadnezzar.
Lebanon Mountains: the land of Israel.
Top of a cedar tree: King Jehoiachin of Judah.

17.4   Land of commerce: Babylonia.
City of merchants: Babylon.

17.5   A young plant: King Zedekiah of Judah.
Hebrew has an additional word, the meaning of which is unclear.

17.7   Another giant eagle: the king of Egypt.
Sent its roots toward him: Zedekiah sought the help of the king
of Egypt against Babylonia.
And now the vine...growing; or And now the vine turned away
from the garden where it was growing and sent its roots toward
him and turned its leaves toward him, in the hope that he would
give it water.

17.12   parable; or allegory.
The king of Babylonia: Nebuchadnezzar.
The king: Jehoiachin, king of Judah.

17.13   One of the king's family: Jehoiachin's uncle Zedekiah, whom
Nebuchadnezzar made king of Judah (2 Kgs 24.17).

17.15   The king of Judah: Zedekiah.

17.22   The top of a tall cedar: a descendant of David.

17.23   Israel's highest mountain: a figure of Mount Zion.

18.10   Some ancient translations who does any; Hebrew unclear.

18.13   Die: prematurely.

18.17   Some ancient translations (see also verse 8) to do evil;
Hebrew from the poor.

18.18   Some ancient translations robbed; Hebrew unclear.

19.2   Your mother: the southern kingdom of Judah.

19.3   A cub: King Joahaz, who was taken prisoner to Egypt (see 2 Kgs
23.31-34).

19.5   Another of her cubs: King Jehoiachin, who was taken prisoner to Babylonia (see 2 Kgs 24.8-15).

19.7   One ancient translation wrecked forts; Hebrew unclear.

19.10   Hebrew has an additional word, the meaning of which is unclear.

20.1   Fifth month of the seventh year: August 591 B.C.

20.3   Mortal man: see 2.1.

20.29   High places: pagan places of worship which the Hebrews were forbidden to use. The Hebrew word translated "High Places" sounds like the Hebrew for "where you go."

20.35   Desert of the Nations: perhaps a reference to the desert through which the Israelites would pass on their way home from exile in Babylonia.

20.40   Holy mountain: Mount Zion, the hill in Jerusalem which formed part of the Temple and palace area.

20.46   The south: the southern kingdom of Judah.

21.10   Probable text There...punishment; Hebrew unclear.

21.13   Verse 13 in Hebrew is unclear.

21.14   Some ancient translations terrifies; Hebrew unclear.

21.15   Probable text threatening their city with a sword; Hebrew unclear.
        Their city: Jerusalem.

21.16   Verse 16 in Hebrew is unclear.

21.19   Probable text Put up signposts where the roads fork; Hebrew unclear.

21.20   Rabbah: capital of Ammon, a country on the east side of the Jordan River.

21.21   Shakes the arrows: when faced with a decision, people in ancient times would sometimes take a handful of arrows, throw them down, and study the pattern in which they fell, in order to learn what to do.

21.25   Ruler of Israel: King Zedekiah of Judah.

22.7   Foreigners: non-Jews living among the Israelites.

22.25   One ancient translation The leaders; Hebrew A conspiracy of her prophets.

22.29   Foreigners: see 22.7.

23.2   Mortal man: see 2.1.

23.4   Oholah: this name in Hebrew means "her sanctuary."
        Oholibah: this name in Hebrew means "my sanctuary is in her."

23.23   Chaldeans: people from a region in southern Babylonia.
        Pekod, Shoa, and Koa: regions near Babylonia.

23.24   One ancient translation north; Hebrew unclear.

23.43   Verses 42-43 in Hebrew are unclear.

24.1   Tenth month of the ninth year: January 588 B.C.

24.2   Beginning the siege: see 2 Kgs 25.1.

24.5   Probable text wood; Hebrew bones.

24.7   The dust would hide it: blood, the source of life, was sacred,
        and had to be covered when spilled in bloodshed (see Lev 17.13).

24.10   Some ancient translations Boil away the broth; Hebrew unclear.

24.12   Verse 12 in Hebrew begins with two words, the meaning of which
        is unclear.

24.23   to; or for.

24.27   Get back the power of speech: see 3.26-27 and 33.21-22.

25.2   Ammon: on the east side of the Jordan River.

25.5   Rabbah: the capital of Ammon.

25.8   Some ancient translations Moab; Hebrew Moab and Seir.
        Moab: on the east side of the Dead Sea.

25.10   Probable text Moab; Hebrew Ammon.

25.12   Edom: to the south of the Dead Sea.

25.13   Teman: in the southern part of Edom; Dedan: to the southeast
        of Edom.

25.15   Philistines: inhabitants of a confederation of five cities on
        or near the Mediterranean Coast, west of Judah.

26.1   Month: the Hebrew text does not specify the month.
        Eleventh year: 587 B.C.

26.2   Tyre: Phoenician city state on the Mediterranean Coast, north
        of Palestine.

26.5   Stands in the sea: Tyre was built on an island about 1 kilometer
        from shore.

26.17   Some ancient translations swept; Hebrew inhabited.

26.20   World of the dead: thought of as an abyss in the depths of the
        earth.
        One ancient translation and take your place; Hebrew unclear.

27.6   Bashan: northeast of Lake Galilee.

27.8   Sidon: a Phoenician city state, on the Mediterranean Coast, north
        of Tyre.
        Arvad: a city state which, like Tyre, was built on an island off
        shore, north of Byblos.

27.9   Byblos: on the Mediterranean Coast, north of Sidon.

27.10   Lydia: in what is now western Turkey.
        Libya: in northern Africa.

27.11   Gamad: location unknown.

27.13   Tubal: east of Meshech.
        Meshech: in what is now central Turkey.

27.14   Beth Togarmah: east of Tubal.

27.15   One ancient translation Rhodes; Hebrew Dedan.
        Rhodes: an island off the southwest coast of Turkey.

27.17   Hebrew has two additional words, the meaning of which is unclear.

27.18-19   Helbon: about 21 kilometers north of Damascus.
        Sahar: location unknown.
        Hebrew has three additional words, the meaning of which is unclear.

27.20   Dedan: see 25.13.

27.21   Kedar: in northern Arabia.

27.22   Sheba and Raamah: in southwest Arabia.

27.23   Haran, Canneh, and Eden: in Mesopotamia.
        Asshur: in Mesopotamia, south of Nineveh.
        Chilmad: an unidentified Mesopotamian city.

28.1   Mortal man: see 2.1.

28.3   Danel; or Daniel.
        Danel: see 14.14.

28.13   You lived in Eden: a figure of complete comfort and perfection.
        Probable text They were made for you; Hebrew unclear.

28.14   One ancient translation I put an angel there to guard you;
        Hebrew unclear.

28.17   to the ground; or into the world of the dead.

28.21   Sidon: see 27.8.

29.1   Tenth month of the tenth year: January 587 B.C.

29.2   The king of Egypt: Hophra, who ruled 588-569 B.C.

29.3   Some ancient translations you made it; Hebrew you made yourself.

29.7   One ancient translation wrench their backs; Hebrew make their
        backs stand.

29.17   First month of the twenty-seventh year: April 571 B.C.

29.18   Launched an attack: in 586 B.C. King Nebuchadnezzar began the
        siege of Tyre, which lasted thirteen years.

30.5   Libya, Lydia: see 27.10.
        Kub: location unknown.

30.13   Memphis: the most important city of southern Egypt.

30.16   One ancient translation flooded; Hebrew unclear.

30.20   First month of the eleventh year: April 587 B.C.

31.1   Third month of the eleventh year: June 587 B.C.

31.2   Mortal man: see 2.1.

31.3   Probable text You are like; Hebrew Assyria is.
        One ancient translation clouds; Hebrew thick branches.

31.10   One ancient translation clouds; Hebrew thick branches.

31.11   A foreign ruler: King Nebuchadnezzar of Babylonia invaded
        Egypt in 568 B.C.

31.14   One ancient translation clouds; Hebrew thick branches.
        World of the dead: see 26.20.

31.17   Probable text And all...nations; Hebrew unclear.

32.1   Twelfth month of the twelfth year: March 585 B.C.

32.17   One ancient translation of the first month; Hebrew does not have these words.
First month of the twelfth year: April 586 B.C.

32.20   Probable text A sword is ready to kill them all; Hebrew unclear.

32.24   Elam: a country east of Babylonia.

32.26   Meshech and Tubal: see 27.13.

32.27   Some ancient translations of ancient times; Hebrew of the uncircumcised.
Probable text shields; Hebrew iniquities.

33.2   Mortal man: see 2.1.

33.21   Tenth month of the twelfth year: January 585 B.C. Some Hebrew manuscripts and some ancient translations have eleventh year, a date (586 B.C.) which is to be preferred.

33.22   Gave me back the power of speech: see 3.26-27.

33.25   Eat meat with the blood still in it: forbidden by the Law of Moses (see Lev 17.10-11).

34.26   Sacred hill: see 20.40.

35.2   Edom: to the south of the Dead Sea.

35.6   One ancient translation are guilty of; Hebrew hate.

36.1   Mortal man: see 2.1.

36.13   Man-eater...robs the nation of its children: a reference either to the poor quality of the soil, resulting in widespread food shortage, or else to the sacrifice of children at pagan shrines.

36.17   Ritually unclean...period: this is based on the view of ritual uncleanness described in the Law of Moses (see Lev 15.19).

37.9   wind; or spirit. The Hebrew word may mean wind, or spirit, or breath.

37.12   Graves: a figure of exile in Babylonia.

38.2   Meshech and Tubal: see 27.13.
Magog: location unknown; perhaps a fictitious name.

38.6   Gomer: in what is now central Turkey.
Beth Togarmah: see 27.14.

38.12   The crossroads of the world: Jerusalem (see 5.5).

38.13   Sheba: see 27.22.
        Dedan: see 25.13.

38.14   One ancient translation set out; Hebrew know.

38.21   One ancient translation terrify Gog with all sorts of calamities;
        Hebrew unclear.

39.11   Hebrew has four additional words, the meaning of which is unclear.

39.14   Some ancient translations those bodies; Hebrew the travelers.

40.1   Tenth day of the...twenty-fifth year: April 573 B.C.

40.2   One ancient translation in front of me; Hebrew in the south.

40.3   A man who shone like bronze: an angel.

40.4   Mortal man: see 2.1.

40.6   One ancient translation deep; Hebrew deep, one entrance 10 feet
        deep.

40.13   Probable text back wall; Hebrew roof.

40.14   Verse 14 in Hebrew is unclear.

40.19   Hebrew has two additional words, the meaning of which is unclear.

40.37   Some ancient translations entrance room; Hebrew inner wall.

40.39   Repayment offerings: see Lev 7.1-10.

40.43   Verse 43 in Hebrew is unclear.

40.44   One ancient translation Then...south gateway; Hebrew unclear.

40.46   Zadok: priest appointed by King David (see 2 Sam 15.24-37).

40.48   One ancient translation and 24 feet wide; Hebrew does not have
        these words.

40.49   One ancient translation 20 feet deep; Hebrew 18 feet deep.

41.1   Holy Place: between the entrance room (40.48-49) and the Most
        Holy Place (41.3-4).

41.3   One ancient translation with walls on either side 12 feet
        thick; Hebrew and 12 feet thick.

41.7   Verse 7 in Hebrew is unclear.

41.12   A building: its purpose is not specified.

41.16   Verse 16 in Hebrew is unclear.

41.17   Verse 17 in Hebrew is unclear.

41.22   Some ancient translations base; Hebrew length.
        The table: perhaps the one on which were placed the twelve
        loaves offered to God (see Lev 24.5-9).

41.26   Hebrew has three additional words, the meaning of which is
        unclear.

42.4   Some ancient translations 168 feet long; Hebrew a way of 20
        inches.

42.9-10   One ancient translation where the wall of the courtyard
        began; Hebrew in the breadth of the wall of the courtyard.
        One ancient translation south; Hebrew east.

42.13   Repayment offerings: see 40.39.

42.19   Verses 16-19 in Hebrew are unclear.

43.1   The gate that faces east: at the front of the Temple.

43.3   Chebar River: see 1.1.

43.7   corpses; or monuments.

43.9   corpses; or monuments.

43.19   Zadok: see 40.46.

43.27   Fellowship offerings: sacrifices in which only a part of the
        animal was burned on the altar; the rest was eaten by the
        worshipers.

44.5   Mortal man: see 2.1.

44.15   Zadok: see 40.46.

44.19   Harming the people: it was believed that ordinary people would
        be harmed by touching something holy.

45.1   One ancient translation 8 miles; Hebrew 4 miles.

45.4   The priests who serve the LORD in his Temple: the Zadokite
        priests (see 40.46).

45.5 Levites: men who performed various tasks in the Temple.
One ancient translation towns there for them to live in; Hebrew
twenty rooms.

45.11 Homer: a unit of dry or liquid measure, about 5 bushels or 175
quarts; so an ephah or a bath would be about 1/2 bushel or 17.5
quarts.

45.12 Shekel: in Ezekiel's time this unit of weight was about 0.4
ounce or 11.4 grams.

45.15 Fellowship offerings: see 43.27.

45.16 Probable text must take; Hebrew unclear.

45.21 First month: the Jewish month that began with the first new
moon occurring after the modern March 11.
Passover Festival: to commemorate the freeing of the Hebrews
from slavery in Egypt (see Exo 12.1-20).

45.25 Festival of Shelters: to commemorate the forty years' wandering
in the wilderness after the Hebrews left Egypt; for seven days
they lived in simple shelters (also called booths).
Seventh month: the Jewish month that began with the first new
moon occurring after the modern September 4.

46.6 New Moon Festival: marking the first day of the month.

46.17 Year of Restoration: every fifty years, all Israelites were
required to give freedom to any of their fellow countrymen who
had become slaves because of debts; they were also to give back
to the original owner, or his heirs, any ancestral land that had
been sold for debt (see Lev 25.8-55).

46.20 Harm the people: see 44.19.

46.21-22 One ancient translation smaller; Hebrew enclosed.

47.10 Springs of Engedi: about halfway down on the west side of the
Dead Sea.
Springs of Eneglaim: on the northwest shore of the Dead Sea.

47.13 Two sections: the tribes of Manasseh and Ephraim, the sons of
Joseph, were each given one section.

47.15 One ancient translation Hamath Pass, to the city of Zedad;
Hebrew Zedad Pass, to the city of Hamath.

47.18 Some ancient translations Tamar; Hebrew unclear.

48.1-7 One ancient translation extending from the eastern boundary
west to the Mediterranean Sea; Hebrew having an eastern boundary
and a western boundary.

48.9   Probable text (see 45.1) 8 miles; Hebrew 4 miles.

48.11   Zadok: see 40.46.

DANIEL

1.1   Third year: 606 B.C.

1.2   Temple treasures: see 2 Chr 36.6-7.

1.8   Ritually unclean: the Law of Moses prohibited the eating of certain foods as being ritually unclean (see Lev 11).

1.21   Cyrus...conquered Babylonia: 539 B.C. (see Ezra 1.1).

2.1   Second year: 604 B.C.

2.4   From here to the end of chapter 7 the book is in Aramic, not Hebrew.

3.1   Plain of Dura: precise location unknown; perhaps south of Babylon.

3.17   If the God...will; or If it is true that we refuse to worship your god or bow down to the gold statue you set up, the God whom we serve is able to save us from the blazing furnace and from your power--and he will.

3.25   angel; or a son of the gods; or a son of God.

4.8   Name of my god: Bel.
        gods; or God.

4.9   Probable text This is; Hebrew Visions of.
        gods; or God.

4.18   gods; or God.

4.27   Stop sinning...to the poor; or Make up for your sins by doing what is right and by being merciful to the poor.

4.29   Roof: flat, where people went in the evening for rest and relaxation.

5.1   Belshazzar: son of Nabonidus, the last king of Babylonia (555-539 B.C.), who ruled with his father.

5.2   Nebuchadnezzar had carried off: see 1.2.
        Concubines: women of the royal harem.

5.11   gods; or God.

5.14   gods; or God.

5.28   Persians: in Aramaic the word for "Persians" sounds like the word for "division."

5.31   Darius the Mede: not named elsewhere; in 539 B.C. King Cyrus of Persia conquered Babylon (see Ezra 1.1).

6.28   Cyrus the Persian: conquered Babylon in 539 B.C. and reigned as the emperor of Babylonia.

7.1   First year: 554 B.C., when he became co-regent with his father (see 5.1).

7.10   The books: in which are recorded the deeds of mankind.

7.13   A human being: a translation of the Aramaic phrase "son of man," which in Greek is the phrase applied by Jesus to himself in the Gospels.

7.15   Aramaic has two additional words, the meaning of which is unclear.

7.22   pronounced judgment in favor of; or gave the right to judge to.

8.1   Beginning at 8.1, the rest of the book is in Hebrew (see 2.4). Third year: 552 B.C. (see 7.1).

8.2   Susa: the winter capital in the southern part of the country.

8.12   Probable text People...sacrifices; Hebrew unclear.

8.14   1,150 days, during which evening and morning sacrifices; or 2,300 days, during which sacrifices.

8.17   Mortal man: a translation of the Hebrew phrase "son of man"; the phrase emphasizes the prophet's humanity and mortality, and his need of God's power to direct him.

9.1   Darius: see 5.31.

9.2   Told the prophet Jeremiah: see Jer 25.11-12; 29.10.

9.3   Sackcloth...ashes: signs of distress and mourning.

9.16   Sacred hill: Mount Zion, the hill in Jerusalem which formed part of the Temple and palace area.

9.21   The earlier vision: see 8.16-17.
        Time for the evening sacrifice: 3:00 P.M.

9.24   Temple; or altar.

9.26   One ancient translation unjustly; Hebrew unclear.

9.27   The Awful Horror: a pagan image set up in the Jerusalem Temple
by foreign conquerors (see 1 Maccabees 1.54-61).

10.1   Third year: 536 B.C.
but extremely hard to understand; or and it was about a great
war.

10.4   First month: equivalent to modern mid-March to mid-April.

10.21   Probable text guardian angel; Hebrew guardian angel. And I, in
the first year of Darius the Mede.

11.1   One ancient translation he is; Hebrew I am.

11.6   Some ancient translations her child; Hebrew her father.

11.17   his daughter; or a young woman.

11.18   Probable text his arrogance...on him; Hebrew unclear.

11.31   The Awful Horror: see 9.27.

11.37   The god that women love: Tammuz (see Ezek 8.14).

11.38   The god who protects fortresses: Zeus Olympius.

11.41   Edom: to the south of the Dead Sea.
Moab: east of the Dead Sea.
Ammon: east of the Jordan River.

12.1   The angel: see 10.5-6.
God's book: see Exo 32.32-33.

12.11   The Awful Horror: see 9.27.

HOSEA

1.1   Uzziah, Jotham, Ahaz, and Hezekiah: ruled from 781 to 687 B.C.
Jeroboam: ruled 783-743 B.C.

1.2   get married; your wife...her; or marry a prostitute, and have
children by her who will be just as bad as she is.

1.4   Jezreel: at this city Jehu assassinated the king of Israel and
all the rest of the royal family, and became the first king of a
new dynasty (see 2 Kgs 9-10).
Jehu's dynasty; or the kingdom of Israel.

1.11   Jezreel: this name in Hebrew means "God sows" and suggests
growth and prosperity.

(171)

2.4-5   the children of a shameless prostitute; or as shameless as
their mother, a prostitute.
My lovers: Canaanite gods.

2.8   Baal: a Canaanite fertility god.

2.15   Trouble Valley: see Josh 7.24-26.

2.16   Baal: this title of the Canaanite god means "Lord"; another
meaning of the word is "husband."

2.21-22   Israel: the Hebrew text here refers to Israel as Jezreel (see
1.4,11).

3.1   The LORD...again; or The LORD spoke to me again. He said, "Go..."
Offerings of raisins to idols: dried grapes were used in the
worship of fertility gods, who were believed to give abundant
harvests to their worshipers.

4.4   Probable text my complaint is against you priests; Hebrew
your people are like those with a complaint against the priests.

4.14   Temple prostitutes: these women were found in Canaanite temples,
where fertility gods were worshiped. It was believed that intercourse with these prostitutes assured fertile fields and herds.

4.15   Gilgal: about 4 kilometers northeast of Jericho, on the west
side of the Jordan River (see Josh 5.2-9).
Bethaven: this name in Hebrew means "house of evil" or "house of
idolatry," and in this passage it refers to the city of Bethel, a
name which in Hebrew means "house of God" (see also 10.8). Bethel
was Israel's religious center (see Gen 28.11-19).

4.19   Verses 17-19 in Hebrew are unclear.

5.1   Mizpah: perhaps the city about 12 kilometers northwest of
Jerusalem.
Mount Tabor: in Jezreel Valley, some 19 kilometers west of the
southern end of Lake Galilee.

5.2   Probable text a deep pit at Acacia City; Hebrew unclear.
Acacia City: probably a city northeast of the Dead Sea (see
Josh 2.1).

5.8   Gibeah...Ramah: cities in the territory of Benjamin, north of
Jerusalem.
Bethaven: see 4.15.

5.11   Probable text those who had none to give; Hebrew command.

5.13   The great emperor: Tiglath Pileser III.

6.7   But...at Adam; or But like Adam.
        Adam: perhaps the place referred to in Josh 3.16.

6.8   Gilead: on the east side of the Jordan River.

6.9   Shechem: a city in the highlands of Israel, some 50 kilometers
        north of Jerusalem.

7.6   One ancient translation burned; Hebrew drew near.

7.7   Assassinated: seven kings of the northern kingdom of Israel
        were assassinated.

7.12   Probable text the evil they have done; Hebrew the report to
        their congregation.

7.16   Probable text a god that is powerless; Hebrew unclear.

8.3   Their enemies: the Assyrians.

8.5   The gold bull: built by King Jeroboam (see 1 Kgs 12.28-30).
        Samaria: the capital of the northern kingdom of Israel.

8.13   Probable text They offer...the sacrifices; Hebrew unclear.

9.1   Baal: see 2.8.

9.3   Forbidden food: the Law of Moses prohibited the eating of
        certain foods as being ritually unclean (see Lev 11).

9.4   Food eaten at funerals: considered ritually unclean because of
        its association with the dead.

9.6   Memphis: the most important city in southern Egypt.

9.9   Gibeah: at this city some Israelites of the tribe of Benjamin
        raped a Levite's concubine; this caused a civil war that almost
        wiped out the Benjaminites (see Judges 19-21).

9.10   Grapes growing in the desert: a most improbable thing.
        Mount Peor: in Moab, on the east side of the Jordan River
        (see Num 25.1-5).

9.13   Probable text being hunted down; Hebrew unclear.

9.15   Gilgal: see 4.15.

10.5   Some ancient translations bull; Hebrew cows.

10.6   The great emperor: see 5.13.

(173)

10.8   Aven: this name in Hebrew means "evil" or "idolatry," and in this passage refers to the city of Bethel, a name which in Hebrew means "house of God" (see also 4.25; 5.8).

10.9   Gibeah: see 9.9.

10.10   One ancient translation I will attack; Hebrew In my desire.

10.11   Probable text put a yoke on; Hebrew spare.

10.13   One ancient translation chariots; Hebrew way.

10.14   King Sharman...Betharbel: perhaps a king of Moab and a city in Gilead.

10.15   Bethel: a reference to the northern kingdom of Israel.

11.1   him, and called him...son; or him; from the time he left Egypt I have called him my son.

11.2   One ancient translation I; Hebrew they.
        One ancient translation me; Hebrew them.

11.3   One ancient translation I took...my arms; Hebrew He took...his arms.

11.4   Verse 4 in Hebrew is unclear.

11.7   Verse 7 in Hebrew is unclear.

11.8   Admah...Zeboiim: two cities which God destroyed along with Sodom and Gomorrah (see Deut 29.23).

12.3   Jacob...his twin brother Esau: see Gen 25.26.

12.4   Fought against an angel: see Gen 32.22-30.
        At Bethel: see Gen 28.10-22.
        Some ancient translations him; Hebrew us.

12.11   Gilead: see 6.8.
        Gilgal: see 4.15.

12.12   Flee to Mesopotamia: see Gen 28.1-5; 29.1-20.

12.13   A prophet: Moses.

13.1   Baal: see 2.8.

13.2   Probable text And then they...bulls; Hebrew unclear.

13.9   One ancient translation who can help you?; Hebrew in me is your help.

13.10   Verse 10 in Hebrew is unclear.

13.14   World of the dead: thought of as an abyss in the depths of the
         earth.
         Some ancient translations Bring on; Hebrew I will be.
         Part of this verse is quoted in 1 Cor 15.55 as it appears in
         the ancient Greek translation, the Septuagint.

13.15   Probable text like weeds; Hebrew among brothers.

14.8   One ancient translation The people of Israel; Hebrew Israel, I.

                              JOEL

2.1   Sacred hill: Mount Zion, the hill in Jerusalem which formed
         part of the Temple and palace area.

2.23   Zion: either the country, or the city of Jerusalem.
         right amount of autumn rain; or autumn rain because he is just.

2.31   Verses 30-31 are quoted in Acts 2.19-20 as they appear in the
         ancient Greek translation, the Septuagint.

3.2   Valley of Judgment: probably not thought of as a specific
         geographic location.

3.4   Tyre, Sidon: Phoenician city-states on the Mediterranean coast,
         north of Palestine.
         Philistia: along the Mediterranean coast, west of Judah.

3.8   Sabeans: a tribe in southwest Arabia.

3.11   Probable text Hurry; Hebrew Help.

3.17   Sacred hill: see 2.1.

3.18   Acacia Valley: identification uncertain.

3.19   Edom: to the south of the Dead Sea.

3.20-21 Some ancient translations avenge; Hebrew declare innocent.

                              AMOS

1.1   Tekoa: about 9 kilometers south of Bethlehem.
         The earthquake: exact date unknown; referred to also in Zech 14.5.
         Uzziah: ruled 781-740 B.C.
         Jeroboam: ruled 783-743 B.C.

1.2   Mount Carmel: in the northern part of the country, near the
         Mediterranean coast.

(175)

1.3   Damascus: capital of Syria.
        Gilead: south of Syria, on the east side of the Jordan River.

1.4   King Hazael...King Benhadad: kings of Syria (see 2 Kgs 13.3).

1.5   Kir: location uncertain; in 9.7 it is identified as the original
        home of the Syrians (see also 2 Kgs 16.9).

1.6   Gaza: one of the five Philistine cities, on or near the Mediter-
        ranean coast, west of Judah.

1.8   Ashdod...Ashkelon...Ekron: Philistine cities.

1.9   Tyre: a Phoenician city state on the Mediterranean coast, north
        of Palestine.

1.11   Edom: to the south of the Dead Sea.
        Their brothers: the Israelites were descended from Jacob, who
        was the brother of Esau, the ancestor of the Edomites.

1.12   Teman...Bozrah: cities in Edom.

1.13   Ammon: east of the Jordan River.

1.14   Rabbah: capital of Ammon.

2.1   Moab: on the east side of the Dead Sea.

2.2   Kerioth: one of the main cities of Moab.

2.7   Probable text trample; Hebrew unclear.
        slave girl; or temple prostitute.

2.8   Clothing...taken...as security: the Law of Moses required that
        it be returned to the owner before nightfall (see Deut 24.12-13).

2.9   Amorites: the original inhabitants of Canaan.

2.11   Nazirites: Israelites who showed their devotion to God by taking
        vows not to drink wine or beer or cut their hair or touch corpses
        (see Num 6.1-8).

3.9   Ashdod: see 1.8.
        Samaria: the capital of the northern kingdom of Israel.

3.11   An enemy: the Assyrians.

3.12   Probable text luxurious couches; Hebrew unclear.

3.14   Bethel: the religious center in Israel, about 19 kilometers
        north of Jerusalem.

4.1   Bashan: a region northeast of Lake Galilee.

4.3   Hebrew has an additional word, the meaning of which is unclear.

4.4   Bethel: see 3.14.
       Gilgal: a religious center about 4 kilometers northeast of
Jericho, on the west side of the Jordan River.

4.11   Sodom and Gomorrah: see Gen 19.24-25.

5.5   Beersheba: a religious center some 80 kilometers southwest of
Jerusalem.
       Bethel...Gilgal: see 4.4.

5.8   Pleiades and Orion: see Job 9.9.
       The sea: the waters above the heavenly dome (see Gen 1.6-8).

5.26   Sakkuth...Kaiwan: gods worshiped by the Assyrians.

5.27   Verses 25-27 are quoted in Acts 7.42-43 as they appear in the
ancient Greek translation, the Septuagint.
       A land beyond Damascus: Assyria.

6.1   Zion: Jerusalem, capital of the southern kingdom of Judah.
       Samaria: the capital of the northern kingdom of Israel.

6.2   Calneh...Hamath: important commercial cities in Syria.
       Gath: a Philistine city, see 1.6.

6.8   The enemy: the Assyrians.

6.10   Verse 10 in Hebrew is unclear.

6.13   Lodebar: this name sounds like the Hebrew for "nothing."
       Karnaim: the name of this small town means "horns," a symbol
of strength.

6.14   Hamath Pass: on the border with Syria.
       Brook of the Arabah: at the southern end of the Dead Sea.

7.4   The great ocean under the earth: the mass of water which was
believed to be in the depths of the earth, the source of rivers
and springs.

7.7   Plumb line: a line with a weight on the end, used to determine
whether a wall is straight and stable.

7.9   King Jeroboam: see 1.1.

8.2   End: the Hebrew words for "end" and "fruit" sound alike.

8.3   palace; or Temple.
       out in silence; or out. Silence!

8.8   Like the Nile River: a reference to the annual flooding of the Nile.

8.10   Shave your heads and wear sackcloth: signs of mourning and distress.

8.13   Dan...Beersheba: the northern and southern limits of the country.

9.2   World of the dead: thought of as an abyss in the depths of the earth.

9.3   Sea monster: it was believed that the sea was inhabited by a great monster which, like all other creatures, was regarded as under God's control.

9.5   Like the Nile River: see 8.8.

9.6   The sea: see 5.8.

9.7   Kir: see 1.5.

9.12   Verses 11-12 are quoted in Acts 15.16-18 as they appear in the ancient Greek translation, the Septuagint.

OBADIAH

1   Edom: to the south of the Dead Sea.

9   Teman: an important city in the southern part of Edom.

10   Your brothers: the Israelites were descended from Jacob, who was the brother of Esau, the ancestor of the Edomites.

11   That day: when the Babylonians conquered Jerusalem in 587 B.C.

16   Sacred hill: Mount Zion, the hill in Jerusalem which formed part of the Temple and palace area.

18   People of Jacob and Joseph: both the southern kingdom of Judah and the northern kingdom of Israel.

19   Philistia: on the Mediterranean coast, west of Judah.
        Gilead: on the east side of the Jordan River.

20   Phoenicia: on the Mediterranean coast, north of Palestine.
        Sardis: perhaps a city in what is now western Turkey.

JONAH

1.2   Nineveh: the capital of the Assyrian Empire, located on the eastern bank of the Tigris River.

1.3   Joppa: a city on the Mediterranean Sea which served as the seaport of Jerusalem.

1.5   lessen the danger; or lighten the ship.
cargo; or equipment.

1.10   and said to him, "That was an awful thing to do!"; or and asked him, "Why did you have to run away like that?"

1.14   You, O LORD, are responsible: God had indicated by means of the drawing of lots (verse 7) that Jonah was to blame and should be punished.

2.2   World of the dead: thought of as an abyss in the depths of the earth.

2.6   Roots of the mountains: the mountains were thought to rest on the bottom of the vast ocean under the earth.
The land whose gates lock shut forever: Sheol, the world of the dead (see 2.2).

3.2   I have given; or I will give.

3.4   and after walking a whole day, he proclaimed; or and walked a whole day, proclaiming as he went.

3.6   Sackcloth...ashes: signs of mourning and repentance.

4.6   A plant: perhaps a castor oil plant, or else a gourd vine.

4.8   wished he were dead; or prayed that he would die.

MICAH

1.1   Jotham, Ahaz, and Hezekiah: ruled 740-687 B.C.
Moresheth: about 37 kilometers southwest of Jerusalem.
Samaria: capital of the northern kingdom of Israel, conquered by the Assyrians in 722 B.C.

1.10   Gath: one of the five Philistine cities on or near the Mediterranean Coast, west of Judah.
Beth Leaphrah: this and other towns named in verses 11-14 were places which an enemy army approaching Jerusalem would attack.

1.14   Moresheth Gath: the same as Moresheth (see 1.1).

(179)

1.15   Adullam: where King David once took refuge (see 2 Sam 23.13).

2.4   Probable text those who took us captives; Hebrew rebels.

2.7   Probable text under a curse; Hebrew unclear.
        Probable text Doesn't he; Hebrew Don't I.

2.8   Verse 8 in Hebrew is unclear.

3.12   Zion: the city of Jerusalem.
        This prophecy is quoted in the trial of Jeremiah (see Jer 26.18).

4.2   Hill of the LORD: Mount Zion in Jerusalem, which formed part of
        the Temple and palace area.

4.3   Verses 1-3 are found also in Isa 2.2-4.

4.10   Probable text groan; Hebrew bring forth.
        Babylon: Jerusalem was conquered by the Babylonians in 587 B.C.
        and its people were taken into exile.

5.2   Family line: the promised ruler will be a descendant of King
        David, who was from Bethlehem.

5.6   Land of Nimrod: another name for Assyria (see Gen 10.9-11).
        Probable text they; Hebrew he.

5.14   Asherah: Canaanite goddess of fertility.

6.2   Foundations of the earth: it was believed that the surface of
        the earth was supported by pillars which rested on a solid founda-
        tion beneath the seas.

6.5   King Balak...Balaam: see Num 22--24.
        Acacia: on the east side of the Jordan River; Gilgal: on the
        west side of the Jordan (see Josh 3--4).

6.9   Probable text who assemble in the city; Hebrew and who appointed
        it. Yet.

6.10   Verse 10 in Hebrew is unclear.

6.13   Some ancient translations begun; Hebrew made sick.

6.16   King Omri and...King Ahab: kings of Israel 885-853 B.C.
        One ancient translation People; Hebrew My people.
        People everywhere will treat you with contempt; or As my people
        you will everywhere be treated with contempt.

7.3   Probable text and so they scheme together; Hebrew unclear.

7.10   We will see them defeated, trampled; or We will gloat over them
        as they lie trampled.

7.14   Bashan and Gilead: on the east side of the Jordan River.

7.15   Probable text Work miracles for us; Hebrew I will work miracles
       for him.

NAHUM

1.1   Nineveh: capital of Assyria, Israel's deadly enemy.
       Elkosh: location unknown.

1.4   Bashan: a region northeast of Lake Galilee.
       Mount Carmel: to the north, near the Mediterranean coast.

1.8   Some ancient translations his enemies; Hebrew its place.

1.10   Verse 10 in Hebrew is unclear.

2.3   Probable text horses; Hebrew cypresses.

2.5   Probable text The officers...forward; Hebrew unclear.

2.8   Probable text Like water...Nineveh; Hebrew unclear.

3.4   enslaved; or seduced.

HABAKKUK

1.5   This verse is quoted in Acts 13.41 as it appears in the ancient
       Greek translation, the Septuagint.

1.9   Probable text and everyone is terrified as they approach;
       Hebrew unclear.

2.4   Probable text will not survive; Hebrew unclear.

2.8   the people of the world and its cities; or the land, the city,
       and those who live in it.

2.17   the people of the world and its cities; or the land, the city,
       and those who live in it.

3.1   Hebrew has an additional phrase, the meaning of which is unclear.

3.3   Edom: to the south of the Dead Sea.
       Paran: probably the wilderness north of Mount Sinai (see Num 10.
       11-12).

3.7   Cushan: location unknown; probably near Midian, the land east of
       the Gulf of Aqaba, or perhaps another name for it.

3.9   Probable text ready to shoot your arrows; Hebrew unclear.

3.13   Probable text completely destroyed his followers; Hebrew unclear.

3.14   Verse 14 in Hebrew is unclear.

3.16   Probable text my feet stumble; Hebrew I am excited, because.

ZEPHANIAH

1.1   Josiah: ruled 640-609 B.C.
       King Hezekiah: of Judah, ruled 716-687 B.C.

1.3   Probable text I will bring about the downfall of; Hebrew the stumbling blocks.

1.4   Baal: Canaanite fertility god.

1.5   Molech: the god of the Ammonites, a people who lived on the east side of the Jordan River.

1.9   their master's house; or the temple of their god.

1.14   That day will be bitter, for even; or Listen! That terrible day is coming when even.

2.1   Shameless nation: Judah.

2.2   One ancient translation before you wither and die like a flower; Hebrew unclear.

2.4   Gaza...Ashkelon...Ashdod...Ekron: four of the five Philistine cities on the Mediterranean coast, west of Judah.
       in half a day; or by a surprise attack at noontime.

2.8   Moab: on the east side of the Dead Sea.
       Ammon: on the east side of the Jordan River.

2.9   Sodom and Gomorrah: see Gen 19.24.

2.13   Nineveh: capital of Assyria.

2.14   Some ancient translations Crows; Hebrew Desolation.

3.7   Some ancient translations they would never forget; Hebrew their dwelling would not be cut off.

3.11   Sacred hill: Mount Zion in Jerusalem, which formed part of the Temple and palace area.

3.17   Some ancient translations give you new life; Hebrew be silent.

3.18   Verse 18 in Hebrew is unclear.

HAGGAI

1.1   Second year: 520 B.C.
        Sixth month: the Jewish month that began with the first new
moon occurring after the modern August 6.
        Zerubbabel...Joshua: see Ezra 5.1-2.

1.4   Temple lies in ruins: plundered and set on fire by the Babylonians
in 587 B.C.

1.9   I blew it away; or I spoiled it.

1.12   who had returned from the exile; or who had not gone into exile.

1.14   who had returned from the exile; or who had not gone into exile.

2.1   Seventh month: the Jewish month that began with the first new
moon occurring after the modern September 4.

2.10   Ninth month: the Jewish month that began with the first new
moon occurring in modern November.
        Second year: see 1.1.

ZECHARIAH

1.1   Eighth month of the second year: October 520 B.C.

1.7   Eleventh month: the Jewish month that began with the first new
moon occurring in modern January.

2.8   Hebrew has two additional words, the meaning of which is unclear.

3.1   High Priest Joshua: see Haggai 1.1.
        Satan: a supernatural being whose name indicates he was regarded
as man's opponent.

3.2   One ancient translation The angel of the LORD; Hebrew The LORD.

3.5   Some ancient translations He commanded the attendants to put;
Hebrew I said, "Let them put.

4.10   Verses 10b-14 are moved here from the end of the chapter in
order to retain the natural sequence of the narrative.

4.14   The two men: Zerubbabel and Joshua (see Ezra 5.1-2).

4.6   <u>Zerubbabel</u>: see Haggai 1.1.

5.6   <u>Some ancient translations</u> sin; <u>Hebrew</u> eye.

6.14   <u>One ancient translation (and see verse 10)</u> Heldai; <u>Hebrew</u> Helem.
       <u>One ancient translation (and see verse 10)</u> Josiah; <u>Hebrew</u> Hen.

7.1   <u>Fourth year...ninth month</u>: November 518 B.C.

7.2   <u>Bethel</u>: the religious center of Israel, about 19 kilometers north of Jerusalem.

7.3   <u>Fifth month</u>: the Jewish month that began with the first new moon occurring after the modern July 7; the month the Temple was plundered and set on fire (see 2 Kgs 25.8-9).

7.5   <u>Seventh month</u>: the Jewish month that began with the first new moon occurring after the modern September 4; the month that Gedaliah, the governor of Judah, was murdered (see 2 Kgs 25.25).

8.3   <u>Hill of the LORD Almighty</u>: Mount Zion in Jerusalem, which formed part of the Temple and palace area.

8.19   <u>The fasts</u>: in the <u>tenth</u> month the Babylonians began the siege of Jerusalem, and on the <u>fourth</u> month they broke through the city walls (see 2 Kgs 25.1,3-4); for the <u>fifth</u> and <u>seventh</u> months, see 7.3,5.

8.20   many; <u>or</u> great.

8.22   Many; <u>or</u> Great.

9.1   <u>Hadrach</u>: in northern Syria; <u>Damascus</u>: the capital of Syria.

9.2   <u>Hamath</u>: also in Syria.
       <u>Tyre and Sidon</u>: Phoenician city-states on the Mediterranean coast, north of Palestine.

9.5-6   <u>Ashkelon...Ekron...Gaza...Ashdod</u>: four of the five Philistine cities on the Mediterranean coast, west of Judah.

9.7   <u>Forbidden food</u>: the Law of Moses prohibited the eating of certain foods as being ritually unclean (see Lev 11).
       <u>Jebusites</u>: the original inhabitants of Jerusalem, who became David's subjects after he captured the city.

9.9   <u>Zion</u>: either the country, or the city of Jerusalem.
       Part of this verse is quoted in Matt 21.5 and John 12.15.

9.15   <u>Verse 15 in Hebrew is unclear.</u>

10.4   From among...people; or All oppressors--rulers, leaders, and commanders--will depart together from Judah.

11.1   Cedar trees: trees are used here as symbols of powerful nations or their kings.

11.2   Bashan: a region northeast of Lake Galilee.

11.4   Shepherd: used here as a symbol of a king or leader, and sheep as symbols of his people or followers.

11.13   Some ancient translations Put them in the Temple treasury; Hebrew Give them to the potter.
        Magnificent sum: thirty pieces of silver was the standard price for a slave (see Exo 21.32).
        Some ancient translations put them in the Temple treasury; Hebrew gave them to the potter.

12.11   Hadad Rimmon: probably a name for Baal, the god of vegetation in Canaan and Syria. When the vegetation died each year, the worshipers of Baal thought of him as having also died, and they mourned his death.
        Plain of Megiddo: a fertile area in northern Israel.

12.11-14   Nathan: son of David (see 2 Sam 5.14).
        Shimei: son of Gershon son of Levi (see Num 3.17-20).

13.4   A prophet's coarse garment: such as Elijah wore (see 2 Kgs 1.8).

13.6   Those wounds: pagan prophets would gash themselves (see 1 Kgs 18.28), and such wounds were an indication of the prophetic vocation.

13.7   Shepherd: see 11.4.

14.5   Probable text You will escape...other side; Hebrew unclear.
        The earthquake: see Amos 1.1.

14.6   Probable text cold or frost; Hebrew unclear.

14.10   Geba: about 10 kilometers north of Jerusalem.
        Rimmon: probably a city some 57 kilometers southwest of Jerusalem.

14.16   Festival of Shelters: held in the fall; to celebrate the wandering of the Hebrews through the wilderness on their way to Canaan, the people would build simple shelters and live in them for a week.

14.20   Even the harness bells: like the inscription worn by the High Priest on his forehead (see Exo 28.36-38).

(185)

MALACHI

1.1   Malachi; _or_ my messenger.

1.3   Esau's hill country: Edom, to the south of the Dead Sea.

2.12   One ancient translation May...Almighty; Hebrew unclear.

2.15   Probable text Didn't God...her; Hebrew unclear.

3.1   my messenger; _or_ my angel.

3.5   Foreigners: resident aliens.

3.6   And so you...lost; _or_ And you, descendants of Jacob, are just like your ancestors--you haven't changed!

3.8   Tithes: the Law of Moses required that one tenth of crops and livestock be given to the LORD (see Lev 27.30-32; Num 18.21-24).